Stuzzichini

THE ART OF THE ITALIAN SNACK

Stuzzichini

STEF FERRARI

Photographs by Deepi Ahluwalia

VORACIOUS

LITTLE, BROWN

Little, Brown and Company

New York / Boston / London

Voracious / Little, Brown and Company
Hachette Book Group
1290 Avenue of the Americas, New York, NY 10104
voraciousbooks.com

First Edition: April 2024

Voracious is an imprint of Little, Brown and Company,
a division of Hachette Book Group, Inc. The Voracious
name and logo are trademarks of Hachette Book Group, Inc.

The publisher is not responsible for websites
(or their content) that are not owned by the publisher.

The Hachette Speakers Bureau provides a wide range
of authors for speaking events. To find out more, go to
hachettespeakersbureau.com or call (866) 376-6591.

Little, Brown and Company books may be purchased
in bulk for business, educational, or promotional use.
For information, please contact your local bookseller or
the Hachette Book Group Special Markets Department
at special.markets@hbgusa.com.

Photographs by Deepi Ahluwalia
Illustrations by Stef Ferrari

ISBN 9780316543903
LCCN 2023938831

10 9 8 7 6 5 4 3 2 1

RRD/APS

Printed in China

Contents

Introduction
The Art of the Italian Snack

Stuzzichini /stuz·zi·chi·ni/ (noun, plural)
Italian snacks served with aperitivo drinks before a meal.
Pronounced *stoo-tzi-KEY-nee*.

THE STORY OF STUZZICHINI

Order a spritz during aperitivo almost anywhere in Italy and you're likely to find yourself awash in an entire spread of composed bites—often served on the house. The word *aperitivo* is a derivative of *aprire* meaning "to open," in this case, the appetite. It refers to the time, typically around 7 p.m. or so, when Italians gather before their main dinner meal. They meet to have a drink and decompress, and stuzzichini, the little nibbles that come along with the cocktails, are the edible component of the aperitivo custom. Almost as much fun to say as to eat, the word nods toward the terms *stuzzicadenti* ("toothpicks") and *stuzzicare* ("to tease"), and the little finger foods have enough personality to get you excited.

Stuzzichini are much more than just typical bar snacks like bowls of nuts, olives, and potato chips. Consider them the Italian answer to French hors d'oeuvres or Spanish tapas—an entire way of thinking about composing tasty bites that keep you coming back for more. They are creative and playful, thoughtfully curated and sourced, and oh-so-delicious.

Many stuzzichini also tell a story, reflecting the personality of their region. Take the Crostini di Estratto di Pomodoro (page 117), a bite that speaks of Sicily's deep tradition of tomato processing, intensely hot sunshine, and passionate, dedicated people; or Crostini al Formaggio Liptauer (page 137), capturing in a bite the Slovakian and Austro-Hungarian influences on the northeastern part of Italy.

Most importantly, stuzzichini are symbols of the culture's deep desire to extend a feeling of *accogliente,* or welcoming, to guests, whether they travel from abroad or from across town. Italy has experienced great periods of turmoil, but a commitment to hospitality, and to caring for guests and community, has endured.

Italian drinking culture is now known all over the world, with the aperitivo and its companion cocktails, familiar no matter what continent you call home. Take the ruby-red, beguiling, and bittersweet Negroni (page 221): It became the world's most popular cocktail in 2022, according to *Drinks International,* and its companion, the sunny, sparkling Aperol spritz, needs no introduction. These drinks, along with a category of digestives known as *amari* and cocktails like the Americano and Garibaldi, have introduced the pleasures of the Italian bar to drinkers far from Rome or Milan.

Yet while aperitivo drinks have inspired bars from Manhattan to Tokyo, the accompanying food culture is not yet quite as well known, and it deserves to be.

BRING THE TRADITION TO YOUR OWN TABLE

Stuzzichini are abundant at local bars in Italy, but you don't have to buy a plane ticket to have the full experience. This custom translates easily to the home environment, and this book equips you with recipes for stuzzichini that are approachable, use simple ingredients for maximum flavor, pair well with cocktails, and help you to offer something delicious to guests without having to re-create the Roman forum. In Italy, aperitivo is a daily ritual and connection point for community and family, though I often make stuzzichini-style dinners when dining alone, so you'll also find recipes that can be translated to the home table for any size group or occasion.

Because they are often offered complimentary with a cocktail at Italian bars, stuzzichini are typically easy to make and economical to turn out. They also often provide a use for leftovers or ingredients that might otherwise become waste. That makes them perfect not just for a bar, but for your own home.

Stuzzichini are a study in snackable diversity. A perfect stuzzichino can be as simple as a plate of toasts topped with vegetables pureed into a spread, as in the Crostini di Paté di Fave (page 119), or as familiar as a staple fried into a crunchy new form, like Cubetti di Polenta (page 178). But many stuzzichini are showstoppers, as impressive as a fully composed

meal, like Bruschette di Barbabietola & Burrata (page 114) and Crostini di Fegatini con Ciliegie Luxardo (page 126).

Recipes appear in chapters based on preparation, like *fritti* (fried bites), *spiedini* (skewers), and *dolci* (sweets). To put together a spread, choose a bite or two from a few different chapters so that you'll have a range of textures and flavors. You'll find notes when something can be made into a more substantial meal, or where substitutions can help accommodate various diets, seasons, or ingredients.

This book includes classic recipes from across the twenty regions of Italy, as well as some of my own riffs showing how customizable stuzzichini can be. It teaches fundamentals, but I also hope you'll feel inspired to get creative with stuzzichini specific to your own life and traditions.

Along the way, I'll share stories about producers and farmers, customs and traditions, the raw materials and environments that make stuzzichini, aperitivo, and Italian culinary culture so special. Because you may want a little conversational fodder to serve your guests, too.

I aim to honor a tradition that transcends language and borders, that captures a custom founded on comfort and care, hospitality and heart.

Salute!

APERITIVO: AN OPENING

The Arrival of Aperitivo: Nuova Comunità

Unlike so many Italian traditions, aperitivo is not a centuries-old practice. Drinking vermouth or something bitter or sparkling can be traced back for centuries, but the custom of an aperitivo hour as we know it is relatively new—with the modern interpretation developing as recently as the last twenty years.

"When I grew up, [aperitivo] was something much smaller than what we have today." This is Lucia Soldi, a professor of Italian literature and culture in

Florence. "It was for grown-up people, especially for men who would go out before lunch on Sundays, to meet their friends at the bar before then going back to the family...a drink with some nibbles."

Today, the vibrant, ubiquitous aperitivo looks very different. So what changed? Aperitivo grew in popularity "in relation with the decline of the economy," says Lucia. In the wake of World War II, the Marshall Plan gave Italy an infusion of cash and resources that facilitated an economic boom. But in the 1990s, a changing political wind resulted in economic and social shifts—including three recessions in the next few decades. Jobs and opportunities became scarce, and more concentrated around the peninsula. This coincided with the age of the internet, and an ability for mobility, both socially and geographically (the *nuova mobilità*, or new mobility).

Aperitivo's popularity grew as a result of this migration, according to Dr. Danielle Callegari, professor of Italian Studies at Dartmouth and certified wine specialist. "We can mark the movement from more rural areas into urban areas, and as people moved strongly toward major urban centers like Milan and Rome to find employment [they] looked for community."

In Italian culture, social needs are as critical to living as economic stability. "You need both food and friendship," Danielle emphasizes, and aperitivo was a way for people who were suddenly far from their families and seeking affordable meals to find both.

Snacking with Purpose

This snack-style dining wasn't just useful for patrons. For restaurants in a culture that vehemently avoids food waste, it was a way to repurpose leftovers. They rolled vegetables into a puff pastry, fried bits of leftover bread or herbs, and transformed pasta and risotto into bites that could be served with surplus sauce, all while encouraging crowds to linger for another drink.

Stuzzichini also helped establishments ensure guests weren't drinking on an empty stomach. While enjoying alcohol is part of the culture, drunkenness is frowned upon, and Italians feel it's generally unhealthy to drink without food.

For some, aperitivo eventually took the place of a full meal. "[People would] go out more often [for aperitivo] rather than to a trattoria or restaurant and having a proper meal. It's quicker, there's less of a commitment in terms of money, time, [and choice] of place," Lucia says. And as the practice spread, this low level commitment presented another opportunity— a cultural introduction.

Bite-Sized Introductions to Modern Italy

Food is "a real cultural driving force," says Danielle, and "a casual, informal way of sharing pieces of specific regional or subregional culture." In that sense, stuzzichini are bite-sized lessons in regional identity. Too timid or cash-strapped to gamble on a full serving of horse meat tartare in Sicily, or Tuscan *lampredotto* (tripe)? Give the classics a whirl with a small complimentary crostino instead, and get a window into what is produced locally, what the people have created, and what the land provides.

And because aperitivo is a practice mostly enjoyed by a younger generation of Italians, it is also a window into modern Italian life and culture—which is dynamic and diverse, influenced not only by the past, but by a very active present, by immigration and evolving tastes—through accessible small bites, in the company of friends.

In the last few decades, tourists have taken note, initiating a vast global exchange. Travelers returned home looking to re-create their experiences, and bars abroad responded. Pretty soon almost every bartender under the sun was stirring bitter drinks— aided by the simplicity of many of these tipples, like the equal parts gin/vermouth/Campari formula for the Negroni, or the 3-2-1 recipe for the Classic Spritz.

All that remains is to spread the joy of stuzzichini!

Iniziamo!
Let's Begin!

QUANTO BASTA— MEASUREMENTS, ITALIAN STYLE

I once asked my grandmother about the recipe for her famous anise cookies. Her response began: "Take a glass of sugar, a glass of flour, a glass of oil..." The "glass" was of unspecified size and shape, and the rest of the details were equally fuzzy. When I asked her how many cookies I could expect, she shrugged. "Depends how big you make them, no?"

Today's home cooks are looking for more specifics, but my nonna had a point. The yield for many of these recipes does depend on how you choose to make and serve them, but most are designed for 6 to 8 servings.

Also in the spirit of much Italian cooking, I encourage you to take an Italian approach and allow instinct and preference to guide you rather than adhering to the letter (and numbers) of a recipe. On that note, you'll see the abbreviation *q.b.* throughout. This is a common "measurement" in Italian recipes and refers to the phrase **quanto basta.** Literally, it translates to "just enough," but English speakers might recognize the similar "to taste."

The recipes that follow are, for the most part, blueprints. Stuzzichini are often created to use up leftovers, reduce waste, or highlight a particular seasonal ingredient or regional specialty, so they're rarely static. Along the way you'll find notes on how to adapt the recipes for your own palate, and primers on prodotti tipici from Italian regions for inspiration. Make a pizzette with local produce. Switch up the filling of a girelle. Bring a memorable meal or flavor combination back to life in the form of a crocchetta.

TOOLS

You can accomplish almost anything in these pages with a sharp knife and a hot oven, but I can't deny that I lean on a few specialty gadgets, especially when they can manage more than one function. My **Ooni Koda 16** outdoor oven turns out a lot more than just

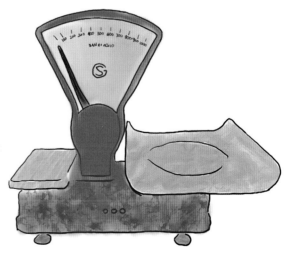

pizza: I also use it to roast vegetables, sear meats and skewers, and get an intense char on something like fett'unta in seconds. I keep a **Ninja Speedi Rapid Cooker & Air Fryer** in constant rotation, especially since it also acts as a steamer, a slow cooker, and an Instant Pot, all of which can be useful when pulling together a stuzzichini spread. I give my dehydrator a run for its money as I convert sliced veggies into crispy chips, create cocktail garnishes, and even invent spice blends, powders, and other flavorings. And lastly, for sorbetti and gelati, a countertop ice cream maker is a handy thing to have around to make spritz-inspired flavors or float cocktails like the sgroppino (page 244).

INGREDIENTS

When it comes to sourcing ingredients, I have some tried-and-true favorites on both sides of the Atlantic.

Italian Provisions

Acetaia Giusti has been making balsamic vinegar in Modena since 1605, so one might say they know what they're doing. Their range of vinegars, aged for various lengths of time and in different barrels, runs from fairly affordable to a very serious investment (a worthy one, in my opinion). All are true expressions of traditional balsamic. Giusti now offers cocktail-friendly shrubs, vermouth, chocolates, and a special-occasion Easter Colomba laced with thick swirls of balsamic and drizzled with dark chocolate, of which I dream once a week.

I love **Luxardo** for the iconic cocktail cherries (more on page 128), as well as their line of liqueurs, not to mention jams and marmalades. When it comes to sweets, **Caffè Sicilia** (based in Noto) is famous for its gelato and pastry selections but ships a variety of products, from raw vacuum-packed almonds and pistachios to treats like torrone and nougat, candied citrus, and a variety of spreads. **Cioccolato di Modica Sabadì** and **Antica Dolceria Bonajuto** are producers of traditional Modica chocolate.

For tomato paste, passata, and salsa, **Pianogrillo** and **Alicos** are specialty producers, and when it

comes to accessibility and reliability, I love **Mutti,** which can be found in many grocery stores.

Pastas from **Faella, Afeltra,** and **Monograno Felicetti** are impressive examples of this Italian craft. I also stock up on **Molini del Ponte** flour from a Sicilian miller working to preserve ancient grains.

I'm obsessed with anchovies from **Testa,** and in Italy my fridge is rarely without a jar of **ROI** olives, both of which can be found from U.S. importers.

American Provisions

While enjoying a rare import is a special experience, the Italian philosophy of buying locally and in season will always pay off, wherever you are. Get to know the folks who grow your food in your community. Try something new from your farmers market. Ask your local pizzeria for a pound of dough. See if your bakery will sell you some of their house yeast.

You can also source incredibly high-quality, Italian-inspired, thoughtfully grown and produced goods made in the U.S. On your grocer's shelf, you'll likely find bottles of olive oil from **California Olive Ranch,** my favorite daily brand. I love to indulge in a bottle from **Brightland,** a female-founded California company that packages gorgeous olive oils and vinegars. **Sutter Buttes,** also from California, and **Texas Hill Country Olive Co.** in Dripping Springs sell exceptional olives that are perfect for stuzzichini, as well as oils and vinegars.

California's **Muir Glen** is a go-to for all things tomato, from paste to peeled whole fruit to prepared sauces.

Sfoglini Pasta in Brooklyn and **Etto Pastificio** in Paso Robles, California, make beautiful pastas. Millers like **Grist & Toll** in Los Angeles and **Janie's Mill** in Illinois are among many sources for fresh grains, and **Rancho Gordo** in Napa, California, is an excellent source for popcorn, polenta, and all things legume.

Edwards Virginia Smokehouse makes some of my favorite products "in the tradition of imported European cured meats," like their Surryano ham (a great stand-in for prosciutto), and **La Quercia** in

Iowa was founded by a couple who fell in love with cured meats while living in Parma, and now provides a version of everything from prosciutto to pancetta to 'nduja—all perfect for recipes in this book.

Cheesemakers like **Cowgirl Creamery** in Point Reyes, California, and **Vermont Creamery** can easily guide you toward a regional replacement for fresh or aged cheeses referenced in the pages to come, and the U.S. has an abundance of other incredible dairies that are more than up to the task.

Fishwife is a female-owned tinned fish curator out of the Pacific Northwest with an emphasis on ethically sourced, sustainable options, including anchovies and smoked salmon.

Virginia Chestnuts is working to bring the tradition of chestnut farming back to the United States with their operation.

For spices, **Diaspora Co.** and **Burlap & Barrel** are both U.S.–based importers who source with great care and prioritize freshness and equitability.

When it comes to booze, Americans are innovating with Italian flavors, big-time. At **St. Agrestis** in Brooklyn, Louie Catizone is channeling his Italian heritage to create a line of drinks that has evolved with the times. Paradiso and Inferno are perfect for making your own Negroni and spritz at home, but the company also sells canned and bottled ready-to-drink versions that are super convenient for sharing. St. Agrestis has even concocted nonalcoholic options like the Phony Negroni and Amaro Falso, and their own version of the cocktail cherry made with their amaro. I'm also a huge fan of **St. George, Leopold Bros., Faccia Brutto, Amaro Angeleno,** and **Matchbook Distilling** among the many emerging distillers and producers out there today.

In terms of trusty retailers in the U.S., **Eataly,** with locations throughout the country as well as an extensive online emporium, was designed to make just about all your Italian dreams come true. **Gustiamo** is a web-based importer of Italian goodies, with a focus on farmers and makers and the "wonderful people dedicated to their land and traditions" in order to promote authentic Italian food.

Cin Cin

Italians are notoriously superstitious. Maybe that can be credited to centuries of conflict, colonization, famine, poverty, and strife. Origin stories may be heartbreaking or harrowing, but their modern-day manifestations feel quirky and ceremonious. Here are some guidelines to successfully raise a glass with the traditional toast, "cin cin" (pronounced *cheen cheen*).

* Toasting with water is a *major* no-no.

* When toasting with multiple guests at the table, never cross arms with another person.

* Look directly in the eyes of the guest with whom you're toasting.

* Spilling a drink can work for or against you. Spilling on a new outfit or tablecloth is considered good luck. That said, losing wine is a misfortune, so dab a bit of the spilled liquid behind your ear to ward off more bad luck.

* Say a few words of appreciation for your food and company, and buon aperitivo!

1

CROCCANTE
Crunchy

For aperitivo, crunchy bits abound.
Popcorn, potato chips, and nuts are excellent
choices, but beyond that trifecta, it's endlessly
satisfying to eat a little something *croccante*
("crisp") along with a cocktail.

Noci Glassate con Aperol
Aperol-Glazed Nuts   24

Popcorn alla Salvia & Burro Bruno
Sage and Brown Butter Popcorn   27

**Biscotti Salati con Mousse
di Salmone Affumicato**
Salty Biscuits with Smoked Salmon Mousse   28

**Patatine di Farfalle con
Crema di Parmigiano**
Farfalle Chips with Parmigiano Cream   30

Cracker di Polenta al Burro Bruno
Brown Butter Polenta Crackers   32

Piselli Croccanti alla Menta
Minty Crunchy Peas   34

Caldarroste
Roasted Chestnuts   35

    Caldarroste di Cioccolato Arancia
    Chocolate Orange Roasted Chestnuts   37

    Caldarroste di Spezie di Zucca
    Pumpkin Spice Roasted Chestnuts   37

Ceci Canditi all'Anice
Anise-Candied Chickpeas   38

**Croccantini di Torta di
Riso al Burro di Acciughe**
Anchovy Butter Rice Cake Crunchies   41

NUTTY FOR NOCCIOLINE   LOVABLE LICORICE
25   40

POTATO CHIPS IN ITALY:
From San Carlo to
Stuzzichini
29

Noci Glassate con Aperol
Aperol-Glazed Nuts

VEGETARIAN, GF

While living in Florence, I spent an awful lot of time at Mercato Centrale—a temple to all things Italian eating. But in particular, I went to regularly pay a visit to a corner vendor with a mind-boggling array of nuts and dried fruit, all ripe for inspiration. I bought hazelnuts for chocolate spreads and pistachios to crumble over pasta, roasted almonds to stuff inside fat dried figs, and pine nuts to make biscotti or blend into pesto. But I especially loved the crunchy, sugar-coated nuts he sold, which I snacked on and brought home to pair with a spritz.

Nuts are integral to aperitivo hour, so I was inspired to experiment with this idea. I'd made bourbon-glazed almonds in the past, and swapped out the American spirit for Italian flair. Aperol adds brightness and depth, while the honey and sugar keep the alcohol's bitterness in check. You can substitute Campari, another favorite amaro or liqueur, or grapefruit or orange juice. Salty, sweet, toasty, and a touch bitter, these nuts pair well with cocktails of all kinds, or can be simply enjoyed as a snack on their own.

Makes about 3 cups

½ cup (100 g) granulated sugar

1 teaspoon (3 g) kosher salt

3 tablespoons (45 mL) Aperol or Campari

1 tablespoon (20 mL) honey

1 large egg white

1 pound (450 g) raw nuts (the crunchier the better: almonds, hazelnuts, or a mixture)

Grated zest of ½ grapefruit (use the remaining rind to make candied citrus [page 200], and the juice for a spin on the Garibaldi on page 218)

Preheat the oven to 250°F / 120°C and line a sheet pan with Silpat or parchment.

In a large bowl, stir together the sugar and salt and set aside. In a separate medium bowl, combine the Aperol and honey, then add the egg white and whisk until the mixture froths. Stir in the nuts and toss using a rubber spatula or by hand until well-coated. Drain in a sieve or colander, then add the nuts to the bowl with the sugar and salt, stirring to coat evenly.

Spread the nuts on the lined sheet pan and bake for 1 hour to 1 hour and 15 minutes, tossing every 20 minutes or so using a rubber spatula to prevent clumping. Once the nuts are golden brown and toasted, remove from the oven and sprinkle with grapefruit zest, then allow to cool to room temperature. The nuts may clump a bit and will be sticky while hot, so toss by hand to break up any remaining candy coating once cooled.

Serve in a bowl to accompany a cheese board, or crush and use as a topping for bruschette, salads, or vegetables—even yogurt or gelato! You can store them in an airtight container for up to 2 weeks, but they probably won't last that long.

note This recipe yields an unexpected by-product that has become one of my favorite pantry additions. After breaking up the nuts, you'll have an orange-hued, bittersweet crunchy sugar remaining. This stuff is sweet gold. Package it up in a jar or airtight container and keep it on hand to use as a finishing sugar for baked goods, a topping for gelato, or a rim garnish for a spritz or similar cocktail. Seriously. It's packed with flavor.

Nutty for Noccioline

Italians are crazy for nuts, which are referred to by the term *frutta secca.* This may seem misleading as it translates literally to "dried fruit," but the phrase is technically accurate; nuts are indeed the seeds of fruit, dried and hardened.

Here's a quick primer on some of the nuts you'll find in Italy. Both domestic and imported varieties are used in savory and sweet preparations, from pesto to prized gelato flavors and about a million other iterations.

MANDORLE
Almonds

Almonds are prevalent in Sicilian cuisine, where you'll find them in pesto alla trapanese, pasta di mandorla, frutta martorana, gelato, and granita, but northern regions use them, too, especially to decorate Colomba at Easter and stud their *torrone*—a chewy nougat treat—during the holidays.

CASTAGNE
Chestnuts

In central areas like Tuscany, these nuts are ground into flour for classics like *necci* (a chestnut-flour crepe, page 55) and *castagnaccio* (a traditional chestnut-based cake), and it's even common to find chestnut in pasta form—either in the dough, or sprinkled throughout a dish for texture. Piemonte is often credited with the candied version, *marron glace,* but these days those confections are found widely (and are mass produced by confectioners like Baratti & Milano as well). During the colder months, it's easy to find a vendor on a city street corner selling *caldarroste* (roasted chestnuts), the recipe for which you can find on page 35.

NOCCIOLE
Hazelnuts

Italy is the second largest producer of hazelnuts in the world, and the northern regions treat them like the crown jewels of their cuisine. They are a key ingredient in *gianduja* (an addictive spread made from sugar, hazelnuts, and chocolate—a preceding cousin of Nutella), which was invented in order to stretch precious and pricey chocolate. You can find hazelnuts in savory items, too, crushed and sprinkled over the utterly indulgent tajarin pasta paired with umami-bomb porcini mushrooms in fall.

PINOLI
Pine Nuts

The oily, spunky pine nut is a personal favorite. It's foundational to pesto genovese, fantastic when used to crust a fish, and exceptional when toasted and generously deployed to flavor an indulgent gelato. You'll find these little guys crowning the top of a torta della nonna, indispensable to eggplant caponata, and sprinkled into sautéed greens or baccalá alla Romana. On the stuzzichini table, pinoli add texture and depth as a finisher for crostini.

PISTACCHI
Pistachios

Middle Eastern in origin, the pistachio has become almost synonymous with Italian cuisines up and down the peninsula. In Sicily, at the foot of Mount Etna, you'll strike *oro verde* or "green gold": The famous Bronte pistachio (which actually has a purple tint) is so important that the entire village comes out to participate in its harvest. Elsewhere, pistachio remains one of the most popular gelato flavors in the country, and the nuts are found crushed into and crusting everything from cannoli to codfish, and as a base for brittles and biscotti.

NOCI
Walnuts

Walnuts' bitterness is well suited to the Italian palate—and the aperitivo table. They're commonly found toasted and tossed in pastas like pansoti in salsa di noci in Liguria or stuffed into dried figs and dates at Christmastime, and then there's my favorite form— a liqueur made from unripe walnuts called nocino.

Popcorn alla Salvia & Burro Bruno
Sage and Brown Butter Popcorn

 **VEGETARIAN, GF**

It was in New York City that I first had a dish of agnolotti with brown butter and sage, at a little Italian restaurant in the West Village. But it was my first autumn in Tuscany, where the small alleyways that snake around any of the region's piazze transform into pipelines for the aroma of this perfect flavor pairing, drawing diners from sightseeing or daily tasks to a candlelit table for a taste, when I really fell in love with the flavor combination.

In Italy, luscious brown butter and sage are well known for being paired with pumpkin or butternut squash pasta in the fall, but here the flavor profile is swapped out for a more poppable, aperitivo-friendly iteration. The butter is an effective carrier of flavor, and the sage infusion creates a heady, satisfying cocktail complement that is delicious on any continent.

Makes about 12 servings

1 cup (125 g) popping corn

3 tablespoons (45 mL) extra-virgin olive oil

3 tablespoons (45 g) unsalted butter

1 teaspoon (5 g) chopped fresh sage leaves

Kosher salt, q.b.

In a large, heavy-bottomed pot, heat the popcorn and oil together over medium heat. As the popcorn begins popping, cover the pot and shake periodically. It should take 2 to 3 minutes to pop fully. (If you have a few holdouts, don't feel too bad; there are almost always a handful of kernels that refuse to pop with the rest of them. I am usually stubborn enough to return them to the pot after removing all the fully popped corn, but you should have plenty if you don't feel so inclined!) Set finished popcorn aside.

Brown the butter in a small frying pan over medium heat until brown flecks form, then remove from the heat and add the sage. Toss the popcorn with the melted sage butter and salt, making sure to coat evenly, and serve. This is delicious still warm, but like all popcorn preparations, it's perfectly enjoyable at room temperature, too.

Biscotti Salati con Mousse di Salmone Affumicato
Salty Biscuits with Smoked Salmon Mousse

Inspired by one of my first experiences with stuzzichini at Caffè Gilli in Florence's Piazza della Repubblica, where for 300 years it has served as a second home for locals and tourists alike, this light and airy salmon mousse makes for an elegant and impressive (and impressively easy) bite.

The salty "biscuit" bases offer textural contrast, but it is a useful recipe on its own. Use the biscotti as a foundation for other mousses or spreads, or snack on them in place of patatine. When making the dough, you can mix in chopped olives, nuts, sun-dried tomatoes, or roasted red peppers (drained); sprinkle with sesame or poppy seeds; top with rosemary; or even season with a bit of turmeric or cinnamon. Customize to suit, and snack often.

Makes 6 to 8 servings

BISCOTTI

¾ cup + 1 tablespoon (100 g) all-purpose flour

½ cup (50 g) almond flour

¾ cup (75 g) grated Parmigiano Reggiano

1 sprig fresh rosemary, chopped

5 tablespoons (75 g) unsalted butter, cut into cubes

1 large egg

Flake sea salt, q.b.

MOUSSE

½ pound (225 g) smoked salmon

8 ounces (225 g) cream cheese

2 tablespoons (30 mL) heavy cream

Grated zest and juice of 1 small lemon (2 to 3 tablespoons juice)

Kosher salt, q.b.

Fresh dill, for garnish

MAKE THE BISCOTTI

In the bowl of a stand mixer or a medium bowl, mix together the flours, cheese, and rosemary, then work in the cubes of butter (like a shortbread or pie crust) until you have a shaggy dough. Add the egg and continue to mix, adding a little water if too dry, until homogenous. Wrap the ball of dough in plastic and rest for about 30 minutes in the fridge.

Preheat the oven to 350°F / 175°C and line a sheet pan with Silpat or parchment.

Roll the dough out on a lightly floured surface to about ⅛ inch thick. Cut into preferred shapes (to serve with the salmon mousse, I typically stick to small rounds, but you can certainly get creative!). Arrange on the sheet pan and add flaky salt to taste (I like a generous amount). Bake for 15 to 18 minutes, until golden at the edges. Store in an airtight container for 4 to 5 days.

MAKE THE MOUSSE

In a food processor, combine the salmon, cream cheese, cream, and lemon juice and blend until creamy. If a food processor isn't available, you can use a sharp knife to finely chop the salmon, then fold in the cream cheese, cream, and lemon juice in a bowl. It will be a bit less creamy, but no less delicious. Add kosher salt to taste. Fold in the lemon zest and dill.

Use a spoon or piping bag to place a dollop of salmon mousse on each biscotto. Garnish with dill and more lemon zest and serve.

Potato Chips in Italy

FROM SAN CARLO TO STUZZICHINI

Bowls of *patatine*—potato chips—are probably the most ubiquitous aperitivo snack. If you've been in an Italian supermarket, you've no doubt found yourself among pristine white bags of crispy patatine produced by the San Carlo company. While these are a staple in bars up and down the peninsula—not to mention in more than thirty other countries—the origin story, like so many Italian classics, is one of family, small-batch quality, and the inspiration one can find in serving a small community.

The story goes that Francesco Vitaloni opened a rosticceria in 1936 Milano and named it San Carlo, after the church down the street. Originally, Francesco was peddling just crispy potatoes, or *patatine croccanti*, as a side dish to his primary fare of roasted meats, fish, and groceries, but the demand grew quickly. Pretty soon, Francesco found his chips in high demand and started local chip delivery by way of his trusty Fiat.

Today, the popularity of aperitivo hour, and the modern, curious palates of its participants, have broadened the market for potato chip makers. The company has expanded its offerings to include chips flavored with tomato, pesto, lime and pink peppercorn, mint and chili pepper, and porchetta (as well as other aperitivo classics like nuts and rice crackers). In an effort to maintain a place at the table, major commercial brands like Salati Preziosi and Crik Crok have gotten in on the innovative flavor game (carbonara-flavored crisps, anyone?). But the increased demand for aperitivo snacks means small, independent makers have a shot at the stuzzichini spread, too.

At home, those new flavors can be inspiring when it comes to customizing an aperitivo offering. Making personalized spice blends is a fun way to express your own culture or culinary style. Even if you don't have the time or tools to fry your own, you can add flair to store-bought chips. Just grab a bag of your favorite brand and spread them on a sheet pan, toast for about 5 minutes at 350°F / 175°C, then toss with your chosen flavorings. I love a combination of lemon zest (about half a lemon's worth), dried basil (about ½ teaspoon), garlic powder (⅛ teaspoon), and a few turns of black pepper for an 8-ounce / 226-g bag of kettle chips.

Patatine di Farfalle con Crema di Parmigiano
Farfalle Chips with Parmigiano Cream

 VEGETARIAN

Before traveling in Italy, I'd never considered doing anything with pasta beyond boiling it, saucing it, and serving it in a bowl. Then I had toasted ravioli with marinara sauce in Tuscany, and then I had fried tortellini in its birthplace of Bologna, where you can order it dusted with powdered sugar to go with your espresso. I even found stands where coils of spaghetti that look like the burners of an old electric stove are fried into little crackers. It is always fun to discover how the people of the peninsula choose to play with their pasta.

At aperitivo time, these crunchy pasta bites can play stand in for potato chips. Crema di Parmigiano is the Italian answer to the American jarred cheese dip, and with loads of black pepper its flavor profile mimics the classic cacio e pepe we all know and love.

This recipe works with lots of pasta shapes, but in my opinion these butterflies (or bow ties, depending on who you ask) are an ideal size and shape for dipping.

Makes 6 to 8 servings

PATATINE DI FARFALLE

8 ounces (225 g) farfalle pasta, cooked to al dente

2 tablespoons (30 mL) extra-virgin olive oil

¼ cup (25 g) grated Pecorino Romano (Parmigiano Reggiano works as well)

Kosher salt, q.b.

Fresh-cracked black pepper, q.b.

1 teaspoon (3 g) red pepper flakes (optional)

1 teaspoon (3 g) garlic powder (optional)

CREMA DI PARMIGIANO

⅓ cup plus 1 tablespoon (90 mL) whole milk

2½ tablespoons (35 g) unsalted butter

2½ tablespoons (20 g) all-purpose flour

¼ cup plus 3 tablespoons (105 mL) water

1 cup (100 g) grated Parmigiano Reggiano (Pecorino Romano and Grana Padano also work)

Kosher salt, q.b.

Fresh-cracked black pepper, q.b. (I like a lot of black pepper here, to give it a cacio e pepe feel, so I usually start with around ½ tablespoon and work my way up)

MAKE THE PATATINE DI FARFALLE

Preheat the oven to 400°F / 205°C and line a sheet pan with Silpat or parchment.

In a medium bowl, toss the cooked pasta with the olive oil, cheese, salt, pepper, and any spices or seasonings you choose, then spread on your sheet pan, avoiding overlap as much as possible.

Bake for 20 to 25 minutes, until browned and crisp. Allow to cool slightly.

MAKE THE CREMA DI PARMIGIANO

In a medium pot, bring the milk to a simmer. In a separate pan, melt the butter over low heat. When fully melted, gradually add the flour and whisk to a roux. It should be golden and fragrant.

Gradually add the heated milk and water to the roux, stirring well with a whisk. Continue to whisk over low heat until the mixture thickens.

Remove from the heat, gradually stir in the cheese, then season with salt and pepper while continuing to whisk, until the mixture becomes thick; it will continue to thicken as it cools. This is best served warm, but can be refrigerated.

Serve the patatine di farfalle with the Crema di Parmigiano or your choice of dipping sauce.

....

notes For even crispier patatine, you can fry the chips. If you have an air fryer, preheat to 350°F / 175°C. Season the pasta, then cook for about 10 minutes, until crisp. Alternatively, for traditional stovetop frying, prepare a deep skillet with peanut oil (which has a higher smoke point and allows for a fast, crispy fry) about ½ inch deep. After draining the al dente pasta (and before seasoning), fry in oil for about 4 minutes, flipping halfway through. Drain on paper towels and toss with the olive oil, cheese, salt, and spices.

You can adjust the thickness of the crema, adding flour to thicken further and create more of a dip, or decreasing the flour by 10 or 20 grams for a thinner consistency, which makes it work great as a pasta sauce.

Cracker di Polenta al Burro Bruno
Brown Butter Polenta Crackers

VEGETARIAN

When I was growing up, my family called upon the pantry staple polenta to stretch a meal, but beyond that function, I had never given the ingredient—a simple, coarsely ground cornmeal—much thought.

Then, one very cold November while I was traveling in the Collio area of Friuli Venezia Giulia to study the local wines, a dish changed the way I thought about this humble ingredient. It was a simple composition—soft, yellow polenta garnished with a drizzle of browned butter, topped with crunchy fried bits of cornmeal, and dotted with tender cubes of a local ricotta-like cheese—but it left me speechless.

I wanted to re-create that feeling and flavor profile in a single bite, and these crackers were born. The nuttiness of the brown butter and the sweetness of the cornmeal make for a satisfying snack on their own, but they're also delicious as a platform for your favorite cheese (ricotta, Gorgonzola, fontina, and goat cheese work best), and pair well with a bitter beverage. They can be dressed up, too, if you want to add spices, herbs, or seeds, and I especially enjoy them with the kick of cayenne.

Makes about 60 crackers

3 tablespoons (45 g) unsalted butter, softened

1 cup (120 g) all-purpose flour

1 cup (150 g) cornmeal

½ cup (125 mL) water (room temperature)

¼ cup (60 mL) whole milk

½ cup (50 g) grated cheese (Parmigiano Reggiano, Pecorino Romano)

Kosher salt, q.b. (I usually start with about 1 tablespoon or 8 g)

Fresh-cracked black pepper, q.b.

Spices like cayenne, fresh herbs like thyme or rosemary, fennel or bee pollen, flake sea salt, q.b. (optional)

Brown the butter in a small frying pan over medium heat until brown flecks form. Remove from the heat and allow to cool until solid but soft. In a medium bowl, combine the flour, cornmeal, water, milk, cheese, salt, and pepper (as well as any optional herbs or spices) with a rubber spatula or by hand. When well combined, shape into a ball of dough, wrap in plastic, and allow to rest in the fridge for about 30 minutes.

Preheat the oven to 400°F / 205°C and line a sheet pan with Silpat or parchment.

On a lightly floured surface (you can use cornmeal instead of flour), roll the dough ⅛ to ¼ inch thick. You can adjust the thickness depending on your preference; the most important thing is that it is consistent for even baking. Use a cookie cutter or knife to cut out preferred shapes and arrange on the sheet pan, leaving about ¼ inch of space between them. Prick the crackers with a fork (once or twice, depending on the size) to prevent puffing during baking.

Bake for 8 to 10 minutes, until golden and crisp. Cool on a wire rack.

Serve with your favorite cheese or a dip like Crema di Parmigiano (page 30), or even top a larger cracker with the roasted mushrooms from the piadine recipe on page 130.

The crackers will last 3 to 5 days in an airtight container, but if they start to soften, crisp them up in a 350°F / 175°C oven for 3 to 5 minutes.

Piselli Croccanti alla Menta
Minty Crunchy Peas

VEGAN

In the springtime, peas show up like little green gemstones in wicker baskets on market tables, and it's always a race to consume as many as possible, as quickly as possible, and in as many iterations as possible. This preparation, however, can also utilize frozen peas, which means that, with the addition of a little paprika and salt to balance and bring out their natural sweetness, these crunchy bites are a poppable way to celebrate any season.

If mint doesn't speak to you, you can also substitute other seasonings or herbs of your choice. Peas love coriander, thyme, tarragon, basil, chili powder, garlic, and onion!

Makes about 2 servings

Extra-virgin olive oil, q.b.

1¾ cups (250 g) peas, either fresh (shelled) or frozen (thawed and patted dry with a paper towel)

1 to 2 teaspoons (3 to 6 g) all-purpose flour

Kosher salt, q.b.

Ground paprika (or other spice), q.b.

3 fresh mint leaves, chopped

Preheat the oven to 400°F / 205°C and grease a sheet pan with oil. (Avoid using parchment or Silpat here; a greased pan will yield a crunchier result.)

Rinse and drain the peas and dry with clean paper towels. In a medium bowl, sift together the flour, salt, and paprika. You can also use another seasoning of your choice, sub all-purpose flour for a nut flour like pistachio or almond for a slightly different flavor profile, or use a flavored oil (like the anise oil on page 38) to get creative. Stir in the chopped mint.

Toss the peas in the flour mixture, then spread on the sheet pan. Bake, turning occasionally, for 20 to 30 minutes, until golden brown. Remove from the oven and allow to cool. The peas will still be slightly soft when warm and continue to crisp while they cool (wait about 20 minutes for best results).

Caldarroste
Roasted Chestnuts

VEGAN, GF

Travel through almost any major Italian city in the cooler months and you're likely to find yourself floating toward a caldarroste vendor in a daze. In Florence, I often purchase my chestnuts from a cart near Piazza della Repubblica, where a friendly gentleman heats the chestnuts before handing them over in a cleverly designed two-part paper bag, one half containing the nuts and the other for stashing the spent shells.

Roasting chestnuts at home brings that incredible perfume indoors. Pair with Vin Brulé (page 247), get cozy, and repeat as often as possible. If you have leftovers, they're wonderful tossed into salads, pastas, and roasted vegetables. I also love them in yogurt as a breakfast treat, or as a topping for a creamy gelato.

(CONTINUES)

Makes about 6 servings

3¾ cups (about 1 pound or 450 g) chestnuts

Water, q.b. (7 to 8 cups or 1½ to 2 liters)

Soak the chestnuts in water for about 2 hours, in order to make them easier to peel once roasted.

Preheat the oven to 475°F / 245°C and line a sheet pan with Silpat or parchment.

Drain the chestnuts and dry with a clean paper towel. On the domed side, slice an X into each. Spread the nuts on the sheet pan and roast for 10 minutes. Reduce the heat to 425°F / 220°C and roast another 20 minutes, until the split shell has curled a bit. (You can also air fry at 375°F / 190°F for 25 to 30 minutes, shaking the basket halfway through.) Remove from the oven and allow to rest. Once cool enough, peel and enjoy—these are best served still hot.

CALDARROSTE VARIATIONS

While the *semplice,* or simple preparation, is most classic, and the chestnuts are delicious as they are, I will admit I have more than one American friend or family member who look for something more when it comes to snacking on chestnuts. Fortunately, they are super adaptable, too, and pair especially well with butter. You can season with salt, pepper, cinnamon, nutmeg, chili, or just about anything else you can imagine. Chestnuts have a firm, toothsome texture and a mild flavor, which means they're a perfect canvas for your preferences. The following are a couple flavored butters to make everything a bit more interesting.

Caldarroste di Cioccolato Arancia
Chocolate Orange Roasted Chestnuts

Chestnuts are a natural fit for both citrus and chocolate, and all three ingredients are significant to the holiday season in Italy. To me, this recipe is the essence of a *buon natale* (merry Christmas).

½ cup (115 g) unsalted butter
1½ teaspoons (5 g) powdered sugar
1 tablespoon (8 g) cocoa powder
1 scant teaspoon (2 to 4 g) grated orange zest

In a medium microwave-safe bowl, melt the butter. Stir in the sugar, cocoa, and orange zest and mix until evenly distributed. Toss with the warm peeled chestnuts and serve.

Caldarroste di Spezie di Zucca
Pumpkin Spice Roasted Chestnuts

Because the latte-loving American in me couldn't resist combining these autumnal flavors.

½ cup (115 g) unsalted butter
1½ teaspoons (4 g) pumpkin pie spice
¼ teaspoon (1 g) kosher salt

In a medium microwave-safe bowl, melt the butter. Stir in spice and salt and mix until evenly distributed. Toss with the warm peeled chestnuts and serve.

Ceci Canditi all'Anice
Anise-Candied Chickpeas

 VEGAN, GF

In Italy, chickpeas are abundant and often incorporated into a dish as a source of protein, or ground into flour to make Torta di Ceci (page 167). In particular, Sicilian cooks have served me some of the most interesting, complex dishes made with these legumes. They pop up in soups and pasta, and even an ethereal hummus-like spread with saffron.

In this roasted form, like the Piselli Croccanti alla Menta (page 34), they are the perfect munchie to throw on the table, enjoyable by the handful. The anise oil is slightly licorice-y and brings a nice balance to the sweetness of the candied legumes, which are creamy on the inside with a slight outer crunch.

In this recipe, the chickpeas are tossed with the infused oil before roasting, but in addition to flavoring these candied chickpeas, the anise oil is delicious when whisked into a vinaigrette, incorporated into a pork marinade, or simply drizzled over crusty bread. Not a fan of anise? Swap in sesame seeds, cumin, or coriander, and/or pepper flakes for a kick.

Makes 6 to 8 servings

ANISE-INFUSED OIL

About ½ cup (60 to 75 g) anise seeds

2 cups (500 mL) extra-virgin olive oil

CECI CANDITI ALL'ANICE

1 (15-ounce or 425-g) can chickpeas, drained, rinsed, and dried

1½ tablespoons (20 g) packed brown sugar

1½ tablespoons (20 mL) anise oil

Kosher salt, q.b.

MAKE THE ANISE-INFUSED OIL

Toast the anise seeds in a dry pan over medium heat until fragrant. Grind in a spice/coffee grinder or with a mortar and pestle.

In a saucepan, combine the toasted anise with the oil and heat over medium until fragrant, 8 to 10 minutes. Let come to room temperature. Store in an airtight container (I often use a jam jar) and refrigerate, leaving to infuse for 24 to 48 hours. If desired, strain out the solids using a fine mesh sieve or cheesecloth. Store, refrigerated, for up to 2 weeks.

MAKE THE CECI CANDITI ALL'ANICE

Preheat the oven to 475°F / 245°C and line a sheet pan with Silpat or parchment.

Scatter the chickpeas on the prepared sheet and bake for 8 to 10 minutes. Add the brown sugar, anise oil, and salt and toss. Bake for another 15 to 17 minutes, stopping to stir about halfway through, until golden brown and crisp. Remove from the oven and allow to cool; they will become crunchier as they come to room temperature. Store in a container with a loosened cover; they're best if eaten within a day or two.

note The infused oil recipe can be adapted for just about any infusion. Try fennel or poppy seeds, thyme or basil, or heat things up with chili peppers. Use the oil for these crunchy chickpeas, or drizzle over crostini, whip into a vinaigrette, or even bake into an olive oil cake to add depth and flavor.

Lovable Licorice

Many Americans have a hard time swallowing the idea that anyone actually seeks out the flavor of licorice. But in Italy, licorice is revered. The root grows in mineral-rich soils in parts of Calabria, where it is considered "black gold," and is a source of deep regional pride. This licorice has earned special status courtesy of the Consortium of Protection of Liquorice of Calabria DOP. It's not surprising, given its significance to the economy of the region, which provides a vast majority of the country's licorice—and in Italy, that's saying something.

Italians turn to their beloved liquirizia not only for its bittersweet quality, which is used to flavor candies, gelati, teas, gum, and more, but for its medicinal qualities. Licorice is considered to be antiviral and anti-inflammatory, and believed to soothe sore throats and relieve acid reflux and heartburn. And because licorice is thought to aid in digestion, amaro producers seek it out as an ingredient in drinks served both before and after dinner. Combined with other herbs and roots in various recipes, licorice makes up a key part of many traditional Italian cocktails and cordials—and is the prevailing flavor in one of the country's most famous alcoholic exports: sambuca.

Fennel and anise—which share a similar flavor profile to licorice—are both common in sweet and savory dishes, from breakfast pastries to puddings, stuzzichini to secondi. But licorice, anise, and fennel are not related botanically. It's the flavor equivalent of a false cognate in language. Anise is an herb in the daisy family while fennel is kin to parsley, and licorice is a root related to beans or legumes.

That said, because true licorice products aren't readily available in the U.S., many recipes for licorice-flavored items call for anise extract instead. When I'm craving that particular flavor, I reach for anise-infused oil (page 38), which I toss with popcorn, drizzle over crostini, or pour over gelato.

Croccantini di Torta di Riso al Burro di Acciughe
Anchovy Butter Rice Cake Crunchies

GF

I have a serious soft spot for crunchy rice cakes. I loved the supermarket kind as a kid, spread with peanut butter or drizzled with chocolate as an after-school snack. When I moved to Italy, I fell in love with a girl who worked on a rice farm, and my love of all torte di riso reached new heights when she presented me with a bag of the farm's organic rice crisps.

I'd seen broken-up rice cakes as a popcorn alternative before, and loved the idea of Italianizing them with a little anchovy butter.

In this recipe, the rice cakes offer a naturally sweet stage for the ultra-umami-rich anchovies, but if you're not into tiny tinned fish, you can also infuse the butter with your choice of flavors: Use the butters from the Caldarroste recipe on page 35 or the infused oil from the Anise-Candied Chickpeas on page 38, or make up your own.

The anchovy butter is also glorious in its own right: Spread it on toast, use it to finish a risotto dish, or toss with pasta and red pepper flakes.

Garlic and lemon also make a crowd-pleasing topping (combine the softened butter with the zest of half a lemon and 1 or 2 cloves of mashed garlic), especially when the finished product is showered with grated Pecorino Romano.

(CONTINUES)

Makes 6 to 8 servings

BURRO DI ACCIUGHE

2½ to 4 anchovy fillets

4 tablespoons (60 g) unsalted butter, softened

CROCCANTINI

12 rice cakes, unsalted (Quaker or other brands work well if you can't find fresh, but try to get your hands on organic if possible)

Fresh herbs, grated lemon zest, grated Parmigiano Reggiano or Pecorino Romano, q.b. (optional)

MAKE THE BURRO DI ACCIUGHE

Mash the anchovies with a mortar and pestle or on a cutting board with the side of a knife. You can keep them a bit more rustic and chunky, or work them into a smoother paste depending on your preference.

Combine the softened butter and mashed anchovies in a medium bowl. Transfer the mixture to parchment paper, use the parchment to roll the butter into a log, then wrap it in the parchment. Chill in the fridge until ready to use.

MAKE THE CROCCANTINI

Preheat the oven to 400°F / 205°C and line a sheet pan with Silpat or parchment.

Break up the rice cakes into bite-sized pieces and spread on the sheet pan. Toast in the oven for about 5 minutes, until crisp and fragrant. They should be warm but not so hot that you can't handle them.

To serve, melt the anchovy butter in a saucepan over low heat, or in a microwave, stopping to stir at 30-second intervals. You'll want the butter melted, but not as "cooked" as brown butter.

Toss the rice cake bits with the melted anchovy butter, as well as any optional cheese, herbs, or lemon zest, and serve. This dish is fantastic still warm, but like popcorn, it's also delicious at room temperature, which makes it ideal for a spread while entertaining or simply watching a movie.

2

RIPIENI & ARROTOLATI
Filled and Rolled

These bites are stuffed, filled, rolled, wrapped, or bundled. This compact style of preparation makes it easy to take ingredients that might otherwise call for a knife and fork and turn them into snackable finger foods.

Funghi Ripieni con Datteri & 'Nduja
Mushrooms Stuffed with Dates and 'Nduja

'Nduja, which counts among its relatives the andouille of France and the sobrasada of Spain, is Calabria's pepper-spiked gift to the world. It is technically a salami but has a consistency like butter and a touch of funk, and is super savory and oh-so-spicy. The dates here bring balance and also give a nice chew, while a bit of lemon brightens up this moody, dark dish.

You can easily make this vegetarian by omitting the 'nduja. To keep the balance of flavor and maintain a kick, add 1 to 2 teaspoons (3 to 5 g) red pepper flakes to the stuffing. Omitting the tablespoon of 'nduja will make the filling just a touch less abundant.

Makes 10 to 15 servings

30 to 40 (about 1¾ pounds or 800 g) cremini (or similar) mushrooms

Extra-virgin olive oil, q.b.

Kosher salt, q.b.

1 large clove garlic, minced

2 tablespoons (30 g) unsalted butter

Minced fresh rosemary, q.b.

1 tablespoon (about 15 g) 'nduja

½ cup (about 60 g) fresh or dried breadcrumbs (preferably sourdough)

⅓ cup (75 g) dates, pitted

½ cup (50 g) grated Parmigiano Reggiano, plus more for sprinkling

Grated zest of 1 lemon, for garnish

Preheat the oven to 400°F / 205°C and grease a sheet pan with oil or nonstick cooking spray.

Clean the mushrooms, then remove and chop the stems; set aside about half of the stems for another use, like flavoring a stock. Toss the mushroom caps with oil until well coated, then arrange on the sheet pan, top sides down, and sprinkle with salt. Roast for 20 minutes, until slightly crisp on the outside but tender inside; drain the liquid halfway through by tilting the pan and using a spoon, or a turkey baster if you have one handy (you can reserve this as cooking liquid for another purpose, like a broth or braised meat). Set the mushroom caps aside to cool. Switch your oven to a high broiler setting.

Meanwhile, in a medium frying pan, sauté the garlic in the butter until it is translucent and slightly browned. Add the chopped mushroom stems and rosemary and cook until the stems are tender and the liquid evaporates, 12 to 15 minutes.

Transfer the mushroom mixture to a medium bowl and stir in the 'nduja, breadcrumbs, dates, and cheese. When cool enough to handle, stuff the mixture into the mushroom caps. You can do this by hand, but a regular teaspoon is helpful to shape the mounds of filling. Sprinkle a bit of cheese over the tops.

Arrange the stuffed mushrooms on the sheet pan and broil under high heat for about 2 minutes, until the Parmigiano starts to brown. Remove and garnish with more rosemary, sprinkle with lemon zest, and serve.

Fagottini di Speck & Formaggio
Speck and Cheese Bundles

 GF

February in the Italian Alps is as cold as you can imagine. Fortunately, the people of the area know exactly how to extend a very warm welcome to guests. When I spent a few days in Val Badia at Hotel Antines, reporting on the area's culinary offerings and skiing culture, I sat down to a very happy stuzzichini situation in the lobby bar: a smoked Negroni, courtesy of a creative and enthusiastic young bartender, a smattering of nuts and cheese, and a pile of thin-as-lace local speck.

Speck is a specialty cured ham that calls home the northern environments of Südtirol and Alto Adige, where Austro-Hungarian influence informs much of the cuisine, as does the cold weather. When prepared according to its protected process, Speck Alto Adige IGP is not only smoked, but often rubbed with juniper berries and bay leaves. Because of the density and intense flavor, speck is often served in delicate slices, which still pack massive punch.

Fagottino translates as "bundle," in this case cheese and other choice fillings wrapped in a cozy little blanket of meat. I'd had this sort of thing before with other cured meats (and you can use your favorite in this recipe), but loved the idea of using speck and a little nutmeg spice for an Alpine-inspired snack. These pair perfectly with a cocktail like the one that warmed me up on that cold evening, or with a simple glass of sparkling wine.

You can also make these with onion and mashed potato filling (like pierogies), with hummus or with another spread like Paté di Fave (page 119), or with just about any other filling you can dream up!

Makes 8 servings

½ cup (120 g) goat cheese

¼ cup (60 g) whole-milk ricotta

Kosher salt, q.b.

Fresh-cracked black pepper, q.b.

Nutmeg, q.b.

Red pepper flakes, q.b. (optional)

Your choice of fresh herbs, spices, chopped nuts (optional)

8 thin slices speck

Long scallions or chives, if needed

Extra-virgin olive oil, q.b.

Honey or Balsamic Glaze (page 83), q.b.

In a small mixing bowl, combine the cheeses and season with salt, pepper, and nutmeg. Add red pepper flakes if using. If you're adding in any herbs, spices, or nuts, include those here as well.

Lay the slices of speck on a tray or cutting board and divide the cheese mixture evenly among the slices, spooning a dollop in the center of each. Wrap each slice around the filling, and gather into a "sack." The cheese should be sticky enough to keep these wrapped in their package shape, but you can tie the top with a length of scallion or a chive, or use a toothpick to secure.

Arrange on a serving platter, drizzle with olive oil, a little honey or Balsamic Glaze, and fresh herbs, and serve.

Pomodori Ciliegini Ripieni con Tonno
Cherry Tomatoes Stuffed with Tuna

GF

Canned tuna fish may call to mind mayonnaise-laden sandwiches that feel distinctly American, but Italians produce about 75,000 tons of tuna annually, and consume about 150,000 tons. That's a *ton* of *tonno* no matter how you sauce it.

This recipe is a sort of Italian version of tuna salad—canned fish married with olives and herbs and stuffed into bite-sized tomatoes—and just one delicious form of the fish to find its way onto the aperitivo table. It's also a testament to why this ingredient features so heavily in the nation's daily life. I first had these bites with a glass of Prosecco on the coast of Lazio, watching the sun set one summer night; luckily, they bring that magic wherever they're prepared.

Makes 8 to 10 servings

20 to 25 cherry tomatoes

3 ounces (85 g) canned tuna, drained

1½ tablespoons (about 15 g) chopped pitted black olives

Chopped fresh herbs (parsley, thyme, marjoram), q.b. (optional)

1 tablespoon (about 15 g) mayonnaise

Kosher salt, q.b.

Fresh-cracked black pepper, q.b.

Wash and dry the tomatoes, then cut and remove the top of each and remove the pulp inside. (Reserve the pulp for another use, like making a fresh marinara sauce, soup, or bruschette. You can even portion and freeze the pulp in an ice cube tray to keep a little taste of summer long after it's gone!)

On a cutting board using a sharp knife, chop the tuna together with the olives and herbs (if using), draining off some of the additional liquid. Place the tuna mixture in a small mixing bowl and fold in the mayonnaise. Season with salt and pepper, then use a teaspoon to stuff the tomatoes. Garnish with additional herbs and serve.

Asparagi Arrotolati con Pancetta
Roasted Asparagus Bundles with Pancetta

At its peak, asparagus is tender, sweet, and grassy. Italians love this veggie with a passion, and even have geographically protected varieties: both white versions (DOP from Bassano as well as IGP from Cimadolmo and Badoere) and the verdant greens (IGP from Altedo, among others).

But you don't have to travel to transform these spears of peak produce into a happy little snack, one that sure beats the hell out of pretzel sticks when sitting around a cocktail table. Crispy, salty pancetta is a counterpoint to the bright flavors of blanched asparagus, and you can even make this a more substantial dish by topping with a fried egg!

Makes 6 to 8 servings

Extra-virgin olive oil or nonstick spray, q.b.

1 pound (450 g) asparagus, trimmed

8 slices pancetta (or prosciutto)

3½ tablespoons (20 g) grated Parmigiano Reggiano

Fresh or dried breadcrumbs, q.b. (optional)

Preheat the oven to 400°F / 205°C and grease a sheet pan with oil or nonstick spray.

Wash the asparagus and pat dry with a paper towel. Bring a large pot of water to a boil, add the asparagus, and cook for 2 to 3 minutes, until tender but not too soft. Remove from the water with tongs and immediately transfer to ice water to sit for about 1 minute (this stops the cooking process).

Drain the asparagus and pat dry with a paper towel. Wrap two or three at a time (depending on the thickness of stalks) in a pancetta slice, rolling to cover most of the stalks but leaving the tips uncovered. Arrange on the sheet pan, leaving space in between each bundle, and sprinkle with the cheese and breadcrumbs if using.

Bake for 12 to 15 minutes, until the pancetta is crispy. Serve warm or at room temperature.

note Omit the breadcrumbs for a gluten-free version, or opt for gluten-free breadcrumbs.

"Cannoli" di Melanzane
Eggplant "Cannoli"

VEGETARIAN, GF

I first encountered these served on top of a very elaborate pizza, and I figured they'd be delicious on their own. It's hard to hear the word *cannoli* and not get excited, even when it's in vegetable form (though, to be fair, I'm usually excited by vegetables anyway). This preparation has a lot in common with eggplant rollatini or involtini, but I love reframing these little wraps as savory cannoli, considering they are also filled with an enriched, flavorful ricotta filling similar to the fillings of their sweeter cousins.

While not quite as easy to pick up and pop into your mouth as sweet cannoli—they require a plate and a fork (or at the very least, a few napkins)—they are equally crave-worthy.

Makes 6 to 8 servings

1 large eggplant, cut into ¼- to ½-inch crosswise slices (using a mandoline, if available)

Extra-virgin olive oil, for brushing

Kosher salt, q.b.

1 cup (240 g) whole-milk ricotta

¼ cup (25 g) grated Parmigiano Reggiano

1 large clove garlic, minced

Fresh-cracked black pepper, q.b.

Fresh basil leaves, chopped

Preheat the oven to 400°F / 205°C and line a sheet pan with Silpat or parchment.

Brush the eggplant slices with oil on both sides and season with salt. Arrange on the sheet pan, leaving space in between. Bake for about 30 minutes, until softened and caramelized but still pliable. Remove from the oven and allow to cool.

Meanwhile, make the filling: In a medium mixing bowl, use a rubber spatula to combine the ricotta, grated cheese, garlic, salt, pepper, and chopped basil until you have a homogenous mixture. Chill the filling in the refrigerator for about 30 minutes.

Use a spoon or piping bag to place a dollop of the cheese mixture in the middle of each eggplant slice. Roll into "cannoli," and use a toothpick to fasten the shell around the filling. Garnish with more fresh basil and serve.

note You can also add pancetta or prosciutto, chopped spinach, nuts, or other herbs and spices to the filling!

Necci con Ricotta & Miele
Classic Tuscan Crepes with Ricotta and Honey

VEGETARIAN, GF

I first encountered necci on a stunning Tuscan fall day, strolling through the Piazza Santo Spirito in Florence's San Frediano neighborhood during the Fierucola open air market. There you can order from a stand where these chestnut flour crepes are made fresh on the griddle and then filled to order, wrapped in a piece of parchment, and handed over as a toasty and warm roll-up.

At home, you can enjoy them the same way, or serve them as more of a pancake. You can even make them blini-style—miniature little discs topped with a dollop of ricotta—for an elegant yet still classic spin. Because they are traditionally a handheld snack, they can be as thick as a pancake—but thinned with a bit more water, you have a crepe.

If you prefer to serve necci as a dessert, you can sweeten them in a few different ways: Add 1 tablespoon sugar to the batter, sifted together with the flour and salt. Alternatively, add about that amount to the ricotta filling. Or if you're looking to really sweeten it up, do both! I prefer the purity and flavor of the chestnut flour and the cheese, making it both a touch sweet and savory. A little drizzle of honey goes a long way, too (go for chestnut honey when available, in keeping with the theme). Don't cut corners on the ricotta. Given that the filling is truly just the cheese, you want good quality to shine through.

Once made, you can freeze the pancakes without the filling. Reheat from frozen either in a 350°F / 175°C oven for about 10 minutes, in the microwave on high for about 1 minute, or in the toaster. They're fantastic to have on hand, and make a wonderful savory snack on their own when topped with anchovies and herbs!

Makes about 1 dozen 3-inch crepes

3½ cups (about 340 g) chestnut flour

Kosher salt, q.b.

1½ cups (350 mL) warm water

Extra-virgin olive oil, q.b.

2½ tablespoons (40 g) whole-milk ricotta

Honey, q.b.

In a large mixing bowl, sift the flour and salt. Add the water incrementally, whisking until creamy. You can do this by hand or with a handheld or stand mixer. The batter should be somewhat loose, but not runny.

In a nonstick pan, heat enough oil to cover the bottom of the pan over low heat. Use a ladle to spread about 3 tablespoons of the batter in a circle and cook until bubbles form, about a minute, depending on thickness. Use a spatula to flip, then cook for another minute, until golden brown. Remove from the heat and repeat until you've used all your batter. (I usually wrap the prepared crepes in a towel on the countertop, which keeps them warm enough for me. You can also keep them in a 200°F / 95°C oven, but be careful not to let them get crispy if you're planning to roll them to serve.)

In a medium bowl, whip the ricotta until creamy, preferably using a hand mixer with a whisk attachment. Place a dollop of the whipped cheese into the center of each crepe and roll into a cylinder. Serve with drizzles of honey.

Seasonality Beyond Produce

These days, agricultural products all over the world are increasingly mass produced, pasteurized, and processed to death in order to meet consumer demands for availability anywhere, anytime. But purchasing fresh and local has an abundance of advantages. Not only is it more ecologically sound, but more enjoyable, too—in-season produce simply tastes better, an indisputable fact if you've ever tasted a tomato in August or a strawberry in June. Shopping at a farmers market in your area makes this simple; all you have to do is look around at what's available to get the freshest foods at their peak.

When it comes to stuzzichini, preparations are often super simple, which means the flavors of each ingredient are on full display. These dishes are infinitely better when their ingredients are carefully selected. And while there is often talk of the benefits of in-season produce, while living in Italy I learned in depth the nuances of *stagionalità* (seasonality) with respect to so many products I hadn't previously considered—that an almond, a batch of ricotta, or even a type of flour will evolve and change in taste and composition throughout the year.

The following are a few examples of ingredients at their peak. I recommend trying to purchase from specialists like butchers and cheesemongers who can walk you through the wonderful world of flavor over the course of *un anno*.

CHEESE

The difference between the same cheese made in the spring versus the fall can be remarkable. When an animal has access to lush, young grasses earlier in the year, the cheese made from its milk will have completely different flavors than that resulting from the same process during the fall, when the animal may be fed primarily hay.

NUTS

Nuts in Italy are a particular point of pride, and harvests are not only major moments of economic and social importance, but they are the best times to use these special products. Although nuts are usually considered shelf stable and thus sometimes forgotten in the depths of a pantry, tree nuts get most of their flavor from their oils, which are subject to quick degradation.

So while they're often enjoyed year-round, there is a particular moment at which their flavors shine through the most. While there is some variation, for most nuts, that's typically from September to November.

MEATS

Much like cheese, the flavors and qualities of meat evolve throughout the year depending on the conditions and consumption habits of the animal. Being aware of those natural life cycles will not only make you a more conscientious consumer, but will enhance your enjoyment. For example, during the points of the year in which cattle have access to more nutrient-rich grass, the resulting meat will be fattier, richer, and more marbled.

GRAINS

Even grains have harvest times, so technically you can consider wheat, rice, corn, and other staples to have peak seasons, too. Thanks to commercial processing, supermarkets are able to stock bagged and boxed versions, but it's worth noting the times of year you might be able to connect with a small supplier in order to taste them at their freshest. Depending on the variety and location, these crops are typically harvested in spring or fall, although the windows have shifted in recent years as a result of changing climate.

Confettura di Cipolle Caramellate & Girelle di Nocciole
Caramelized Onion Jam and Hazelnut Girelle

VEGETARIAN

Onions and balsamic vinegar were made for each other. When you cook them down into an addictive jam, you can get plenty of satisfaction by pairing it with a good cheese, or simply eating it off a spoon. But when the jam is rolled into pinwheels along with crunchy hazelnuts, the buttery pastry and crunch factor keep you coming back for more.

While balsamic vinegar is a geographically protected product exclusive to Modena and Reggio Emilia, you can find prized onions all over the peninsula. Among the red variety, the most famous is the cipolla rossa di Tropea Calabria, which is known for its delicately sweet and herbaceous flavor. This onion, referred to as *la Regina Rossa* or "the Red Queen," is so much a part of Calabrese culture that not only do residents eat it raw by itself, but also in and on everything from pizza to gelato. (Yes, really!)

You can use a local variety of your own choosing, but taste the onion for sweetness first, as you may want to adjust the sugar a bit up or down. You can make this dish vegan-friendly by swapping out the honey for an alternate sweetener (maple syrup is a delightful shift in flavor!) and omitting the cheese.

Makes about 20 girelle

CONFETTURA DI CIPOLLE CARAMELLATE

Extra-virgin olive oil, q.b.

4 to 5 medium (about 1 pound or 450 g) sweet red onions, thinly sliced (on a mandoline, if available), 2 to 3 cups

2 large cloves garlic, minced

¾ cup (180 mL) balsamic vinegar

½ cup (100 g) granulated sugar

¼ cup (50 g) packed brown sugar

2 tablespoons (40 mL) honey

3 tablespoons (30 g) raisins (optional)

Kosher salt, q.b.

Fresh-cracked black pepper, q.b.

MAKE THE CONFETTURA DI CIPOLLE CARAMELLATE

Heat the oil in a medium saucepan over medium heat. Add the onions and garlic and cook until fragrant and browned. Add the balsamic and cook down for 6 to 8 minutes.

Lower the heat, add the sugars and the honey, and stir until dissolved. Add the raisins and simmer, stirring occasionally, for another 45 minutes or so, until reduced to the thickness of marmalade. Season with salt and pepper. Refrigerate any leftovers in a jar or other airtight container for up to 1 month.

(CONTINUES)

GIRELLE

1 sheet puff pastry, 9x9 inches (23x23 cm), thawed and cut in half to make two pieces

6 tablespoons (120 g) Caramelized Onion Jam

¼ cup (about 55 g) shredded caciocavallo (provolone, mozzarella, and scamorza are good alternatives)

¼ cup (35 g) toasted crushed hazelnuts

MAKE THE GIRELLE

On a lightly floured surface, roll out the pastry dough pieces to about ⅛ inch thick. Lay each piece on one piece of parchment, then spread the onion jam all the way to the edges of the pastry on the long sides,

leaving a half inch bare along the short sides. Sprinkle the cheese and crushed hazelnuts over the jam. Starting from a long side, use the parchment paper to help roll each piece into a log (with the mixture inside). Chill the logs in the refrigerator for about 20 minutes (this will make them easier to slice).

Preheat the oven to 400°F / 205°C and line a sheet pan with Silpat or parchment.

Slice each roll into about ten ½-inch-thick rounds. Arrange the girelle on the lined sheet pan, allowing space in between as they will spread a bit. Bake for 16 to 18 minutes, or until golden and puffed. Serve warm or at room temperature.

Chicories in Aperitivo Culture

I have long loved radicchio, and chicories of all kinds for that matter, and they have a deep place in Italy's culinary culture and history. And yet, with all that is ancient in Italy, it's still possible to run into something entirely new—sometimes in the most unexpected places. For me, one such place was a truck stop along the autostrada, somewhere between the Dolomites and Tuscany, on a winter day. I paused for fuel and an espresso, but there, arranged among the Prosecco and Nebbiolo (in Italy even gas stations sell wine and liquor), was a display of Divo Rosso, a liqueur the color of ruby slippers.

I never pass up a chance to try a novel booze, and I learned that this liquid gets its eye-catching hue from radicchio rosso di Treviso IGP. In fact, according to the company website, every liter of this liquor is infused with 500 grams of the precious produce. I took it home and found it to be unusual but delicious: earthy with notes of grapefruit bitterness and an almost hibiscus flower–like tartness, wonderful in a spritz, as a Negroni twist, and simply on ice as an aperitivo. When I dug further into the roots of this drink, I learned that there are a whole lot of alcohols out there that rely on chicories, not unlike the artichoke-inspired international favorite, Cynar.

It was a fun reminder that Italians are always experimenting with their most prized ingredients, but even in their natural, chewable form, chicories like radicchio make a perfect aperitivo addition. Naturally bitter and medicinal, they're known for their detoxifying, antibacterial, and anti-inflammatory properties, and they're packed with antioxidants. They are also perfectly pro-stuzzichini, as they're considered an appetite stimulant and naturally pair with (or serve as inspiration for) bitter drinks.

There are countless varieties, but a few of the most famous are the following:

RADICCHIO DI CASTELFRANCO VENETO,
from Padua, Venice, Treviso (Veneto)
A prized hybrid between radicchio di Treviso and escarole, this autumnal beauty has pale yellow leaves with red speckles. Its flavor is on the milder, sweeter side of bitter. In fact, it's even a key ingredient in a very unusual dessert made with ricotta and chocolate, known as sformato di radicchio al domino.

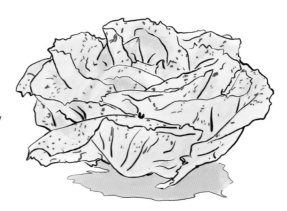

ROSA DI GORIZIA, from Collio (Friuli Venezia Giulia)
A winter chicory, available December to February, this is a small variety that looks a lot like a red rose (hence the name), and would be just as at home in a vase on the table as it would as the centerpiece of a meal or aperitivo spread. Its unique, bittersweet flavor is thoroughly enjoyable raw with just a drizzle of peppery olive oil, and it has also inspired a grappa and amaro made in the area.

RADICCHIO DI VERONA,
from Verona, Vicenza, Padua (Veneto)
RADICCHIO DI CHIOGGIA,
from Venice, Padua, Rovigo (Veneto)
Probably the most recognizable of the bunch, these two varieties are similar in look and flavor (di Verona is more tightly packed and bulbous; di Chioggia a bit looser). They're both beautifully, deeply red and often intensely bitter. Braising, grilling, and roasting soften their flavor, but if you're like me, you might just enjoy their powerful punch raw in a salad, with a simple dose of anchovy-garlic dressing and a squeeze of lemon.

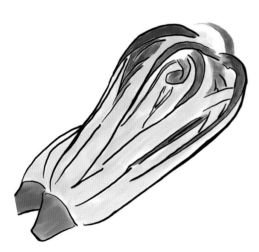

RADICCHIO ROSSO DI TREVISO,
from Treviso, Padua, Venice (Veneto)
Its unique appearance calls to mind long fingers with painted nails. The sturdy, striated leaves are white at the base, tinting gradually into a garnet tip that twists and curls, becoming more delicate and soft along the way. There are so many textures and flavors here that you can make a really interesting salad simply by chopping up this single piece of produce and serving it raw with a simple vinaigrette or bagna cauda (an anchovy-based Piemontese condimento), but it also stands up well when grilled, topped with crunchy nuts and salty cheese, and drizzled with honey.

Girelle di Radicchio Brasato al Vermouth con Arancia & Cipolla Rossa

Vermouth-Braised Radicchio Girelle with Orange and Red Onion

VEGETARIAN

This recipe is a mash-up of experiences. I found radicchio girelle on a stuzzichini buffet in Alta Badia one winter, and, later, an orange, red onion, and vermouth-braised version of chicory as a *contorno* (a side dish) at a Florentine restaurant that blew me away. It seemed natural to combine them.

Sweet red onion, bright acidic orange, and buttery pastry temper the bitter chicory bite here, and the color and flavor profile make these girelle a perfect pairing with a Campari and soda or a Negroni with a twist of orange.

Makes about 20 girelle

1 sheet puff pastry, 9x9 inches (23x23 cm), thawed and cut in half to make two pieces

Extra-virgin olive oil, q.b.

1 small red onion, thinly sliced

1 large clove garlic, minced

4 to 5 cups (about ½ pound or 225 g) roughly chopped radicchio

¼ cup (60 mL) sweet vermouth

3½ ounces (scant ½ cup or 100 g) grated or cubed Taleggio cheese

⅓ cup (40 g) grated Grana Padano

Grated zest of 1 orange

Kosher salt, q.b.

Fresh-cracked black pepper, q.b.

⅓ cup (40 g) toasted unsalted walnuts (optional)

On a lightly floured surface, roll out the pastry dough to about ⅛ inch thick. Lay each piece on one piece of parchment paper.

Heat enough oil to cover the bottom of a large frying pan over medium heat. Add the onion and garlic and sauté until fragrant and translucent. Add the radicchio and cook until softened and browned, about 8 minutes. Add the vermouth and continue to cook until the liquid is absorbed. Let cool.

Transfer the radicchio mixture to a food processor. Add the cheeses and zest, season with salt and pepper, and blend. You can also do this by hand with a sharp knife, which will yield a less creamy and more rustic version.

Spread the radicchio mixture evenly over the pastry pieces all the way to the edges on the long sides and leaving ½ inch bare along the short sides. Sprinkle the walnuts (if using) across the top. Starting from a long side, use the parchment to help roll each piece into a log (with the mixture inside). Freeze for about 40 minutes (this will make them easier to slice).

Preheat the oven to 400°F / 205°C and line a sheet pan with Silpat or parchment.

Slice each roll into about ten ½-inch-thick rounds. Arrange the girelle on the lined sheet pan, allowing space in between as they will spread a bit. Bake for 16 to 18 minutes, until golden and puffed.

Indivia con Crema di Gorgonzola Dolce, Mela & Noce
Endive with Sweet Gorgonzola Cream, Apple, and Walnut

 VEGETARIAN, GF

Endive, another chicory, is not only delicious, but plays double duty as both ingredient and serving vessel. Washed and peeled, its leaves are sturdy enough to support a filling or a dip, and I first enjoyed them this way at Lilia in Brooklyn, where chef Missy Robbins makes a bagna cauda (a garlicky anchovy sauce) that is to die for and presents it with a selection of beautiful produce. Later, when I traveled through Italy, it was easy to see the inspiration as I found endive put to work in so many similarly simple dishes.

This particular stuzzichino is one of my favorite examples of Italian cuisine. There is no lengthy shopping list. No cooking. No manipulation of ingredients beyond a bit of chopping. There is just an understanding that quality ingredients, constructed thoughtfully, will almost always be a success. That means it's also a blueprint that can be adapted endlessly. You can swap out the Gorgonzola for goat cheese, walnuts for hazelnuts, apples for pears, Balsamic Glaze for honey. Use what's fresh, what's on hand, and what inspires you, and you'll have a restaurant-worthy snack in no time.

Makes 6 servings

6 endive leaves

⅓ cup (35 to 40 g) crumbled Gorgonzola

¼ cup (50 g) chopped apple

2 to 2½ tablespoons (about 20 g) walnuts, chopped

Balsamic Glaze (page 83), q.b. (for drizzling)

Wash the endive leaves and pat dry with a paper towel. Arrange on a platter or serving tray and layer the filling: first cheese, then fruit, then a sprinkle of nuts. Drizzle with vinegar and serve.

"Cannoli" Salati con Crema di Piselli
Salty "Cannoli" with Green Pea Cream

VEGETARIAN, GF

The functions of cheese in Italy are endless, but the first time I saw grated Parmigiano Reggiano manipulated into "cannoli" shells in a winery's tasting room in Sicily, I was filled with pride for Italian ingenuity.

In this dish, the salty vessels are filled with a sweet pea–ricotta cream and pressed into crunchy pistachios. It is one of those smack-your-forehead preparations that makes such logical sense, it should be studied as an archetype of balanced flavors and textures.

Makes 6 servings

CANNOLI SALATI

About 1½ cups (about 150 g) grated cheese (preferably Grana Padano, pecorino, or Parmigiano Reggiano; a blend also works)

CREMA DI PISELLI

Extra-virgin olive oil, q.b.

2 large cloves garlic, minced

2 cups (300 g) fresh peas (frozen work, too—no need to thaw)

Kosher salt, q.b.

Fresh-cracked black pepper, q.b.

½ cup (120 g) whole-milk ricotta

⅔ cup (about 60 g) grated cheese (preferably Grana Padano, pecorino, or Parmigiano Reggiano; a blend also works)

1 teaspoon (about 10 g) minced fresh basil leaves

1 teaspoon (about 10 g) minced fresh mint leaves

Pistachios, crushed, q.b.

MAKE THE CANNOLI SALATI

Preheat the oven to 400°F / 205°C and line a sheet pan with Silpat or parchment.

Place a 5-inch biscuit cutter on the lined sheet, drop about 3½ tablespoons (20 g) of the grated cheese inside the biscuit cutter and spread evenly within the circle. Repeat five times, allowing some spacing between shells. Bake for 5 to 7 minutes, until golden brown.

Let the cheese cool slightly, 1 to 2 minutes, until you can handle the rounds but they're still pliable. Wrap each around a 5-inch cannoli tube (see Note) to form shells. Set aside and allow to cool completely while you make the filling. The unfilled shells will last 2 to 3 days in an airtight container.

MAKE THE CREMA DI PISELLI

In a medium saucepan over medium heat, heat enough oil to cover the bottom of the pan. Add the garlic and cook until browned (but be careful not to burn!). Add the peas, season with salt and pepper, and cook until the peas are tender but not soft, about 3 minutes. Remove from the heat and allow to cool a bit.

In a food processor, combine the peas, ricotta, grated cheese, basil, and mint. Drizzle in about 2 tablespoons olive oil and pulse until well combined and creamy. You can also do this by hand with a sharp knife and a rough chop, for a slightly less creamy and more rustic version. Add more cheese to thicken or more oil to thin if needed. Chill in the refrigerator for about 30 minutes.

ASSEMBLE THE CANNOLI

Transfer the pea filling to a pastry or storage bag (cutting the tip to create an opening). Pipe the filling into your shells, press the exposed ends into the crushed pistachio, and serve. Once filled, it's best to serve as soon as possible as the shells will lose some of their crispness, but you can store the filling separately in an airtight container for 3 to 5 days.

....

note If you don't have a cannoli tube, you can use a clean curtain rod or broom handle. (Wrap plastic wrap around the part you plan to use!)

Fichi al Forno
Oven Roasted Figs

VEGETARIAN, GF

In the course of history, figs have shown up in mythological stories and museum sculptures, poetic stanzas and musical masterpieces. Today, they inspire just as widely, and in the culinary arts can be found in everything from jam and mostarda to savory dishes like roasted pork and duck, or converted into sweet gelato, or baked into biscotti or panforte.

But this might just be my favorite iteration: These figs are prepared simply, allowing their natural flavors and sugars to concentrate in the oven. Fill with sharp cheese, roast, and then garnish with honey, herbs, and crunchy nuts. I'd be surprised if you don't pen a sonnet or two yourself after a serving.

Makes 4 stuffed figs

4 large figs (ripe, but still firm)

About ½ cup (100 to 120 g) goat cheese (or blue cheese)

Kosher salt, q.b.

Fresh-cracked black pepper, q.b.

Chopped fresh herbs (thyme and/or basil work well), for garnish

About 1½ tablespoons (10 to 12 g) sliced almonds or pine nuts, toasted, for garnish

1 tablespoon (20 mL) honey

Preheat the oven to 400°F / 205°C and line a sheet pan with Silpat or parchment.

Wash the figs and dry with a paper towel, then cut an X into the top of each, separating the fruit into four sections but not fully cutting them into pieces. In a small bowl, season the cheese with a bit of salt and pepper, then spoon into the opening of each fig. Arrange on the sheet pan and bake for 10 to 12 minutes, until the cheese is bubbly and browned. Cool, then top with the herbs, sprinkle with the nuts, drizzle with honey, and serve with toast.

Albicocche al Forno
Oven Roasted Apricots

VEGETARIAN, GF

Apricots enjoy an almost heroic status in Italy, where you're likely to find their bright and tangy presence in a marmalade nestled comfortably inside a *cornetto* (a classic Italian brioche breakfast pastry) in almost any bar, every morning. And while they're delicious fresh, dried, or jammed, I adore this snackable version.

These 'cots can easily be made more savory or sweet, depending on your mood. Top with hot pepper and salty nuts, or try cinnamon, a dusting of powdered sugar, or a drizzle of honey. You can even omit the cheese mixture and serve with gelato.

Makes 4 roasted apricots

4 apricots

1 tablespoon (15 g) unsalted butter, melted

1 tablespoon (12 g) packed brown sugar

About ½ cup (100 to 120 g) whole-milk ricotta

Fresh marjoram and/or basil leaves, julienned, q.b.

1 tablespoon (15 mL) light rum (optional)

Preheat the oven to 400°F / 205°C and line a sheet pan with Silpat or parchment.

Wash the apricots and dry with a paper towel, then cut each in half and remove the pit. Place the halves face up on the sheet pan, leaving space in between. Brush with the melted butter and sprinkle evenly with the brown sugar. Bake for 12 to 15 minutes, until the sugar is a bit bubbly. Remove from the oven and allow to cool slightly.

In the meantime, prepare the cheese mixture. Combine the ricotta with the herbs in a small bowl. If using rum, add that here, too.

Once the fruit has cooled, distribute the cheese mixture among the apricots, filling the cavities. Serve still warm or at room temperature. You can even store these in the fridge and enjoy chilled in the summer.

Cestini di Prosciutto con Melone & Burrata Ripiene
Prosciutto Baskets with Melon and Burrata

GF

Prosciutto crudo is a common pairing with fresh cantaloupe and mozzarella, but it's usually more of a fork-and-knife kind of food. I was looking for ways to make it more snackable when I came across prosciutto baskets in an Italian bar (there, filled with baked cheese and herbs, which was also delicious).

This recipe twists the original prosciutto e melone pairing ever so slightly, baking the meat into a crisp, convenient serving vessel, and bumping out mozzarella for its extra creamy cousin, burrata, which provides a silky, creamy counterpoint to the crunchy, salty meat. It's all married together by the naturally bright and acidic melon. No fork and knife required.

A big part of the balance in this bite is the sweetness of the melon. Taste the fruit, and if you feel it's not quite sweet enough, a drizzle of honey will get the job done—and is a delightful option either way!

Makes 12 servings

12 strips prosciutto

9 ounces (250 g) burrata, roughly chopped

1½ cups (about ⅓ to ½ pound or 150 to 225 g) cubed melon (cantaloupe is traditional, but a sweet honeydew or even a pineapple works well)

Fresh basil or mint leaves (or a combination), julienned, q.b.

Honey, q.b. (optional)

Preheat the oven to 375°F / 190°C and spray a mini muffin tin with nonstick spray.

Cut the prosciutto strips in half and use to line 12 muffin tin cavities (covering bottoms and sides). You can rip slices into smaller pieces if you need to accommodate any holes. Bake for 8 to 10 minutes, until the prosciutto is crisp, then remove from oven and allow to cool completely.

In the meantime, use a rubber spatula to combine the burrata and melon in a medium mixing bowl with the herbs until well mixed. If using, add honey here, to taste. Once the cups are cooled, remove from the pan by hand. Distribute the cheese and fruit filling among the cups, garnish with more herbs, and serve.

3

STUZZICADENTI, PALLINI & SPIEDINI

Toothpicks, Balls, and Skewers

These recipes celebrate stuzzichini's
relationship to the humble toothpick
(or stuzzicadenti). Here you'll find bites
you can skewer, spear, and otherwise pierce
with a stick of any sort.

Capra & Grana Pallini con Melograno & Arancia

Goat Cheese and Grana Padano Balls with Pomegranate and Orange

 VEGETARIAN, GF

This combination of sweet and creamy, sharp and salty cheeses rolled in crunchy, bright seeds and lifted by zippy citrus zest makes these little balls tough to stop eating.

Pomegranate and orange are both such festive flavors, and they tend to pop up in Italy especially during the holiday season. I associate these little bites with Christmas parties and Italian-style mulled wine (Vin Brulé, page 247), but they are very customizable based on which fruits are in season.

Makes 20 to 25 balls

1 cup (220 g) goat cheese
(or ricotta or Gorgonzola)

½ cup (120 g) mascarpone

½ cup (50 g) grated cheese
(Parmigiano Reggiano, Pecorino
Romano, Grana Padano)

Grated zest of 1 orange

Nutmeg (or other spice of choice),
q.b., optional

Chopped prosciutto (or other
cured meat), q.b., optional

¼ cup (35 g) chopped nuts
(pistachio, almond, walnut),
for rolling

¼ cup (50 g) pomegranate seeds
(or dried cherries or raisins),
for rolling

Arugula or other greens,
for serving

In a medium bowl, combine all the cheeses and mix in orange zest until you have a homogenous cream. If you like, add spices and/or meat. Chill the mixture in the refrigerator until firm, so you can handle it.

Form into balls, 1 to 1½ tablespoons in size (a little smaller than a Ping-Pong ball). You can do this freehand, wetting your hands a bit so the mixture doesn't stick, or use a cookie dropper or similar. Then roll in your chosen toppings. Chill for about 2 hours. Serve with toothpicks over arugula or other greens.

note You can also bread and fry these for a crunchy, gooey version! Freeze the balls for about 30 minutes, then prepare a breading station: one dish with flour or cornmeal (or a combination), a second dish with a beaten egg, and a third dish with breadcrumbs or panko. Roll each ball first in flour, then egg, then coat with breadcrumbs. Fry in about 1 inch hot peanut oil (about 360°F / 180°C) for about 2 minutes, rolling them about halfway through to ensure even frying, until golden brown and crisp. Drain on paper towels. You can also use an air fryer set to 400°F / 205°C. Spray the fryer basket with nonstick spray and air fry the coated balls for 4 to 5 minutes, until crisp and golden. Serve hot just as they are, or drizzle with honey and a squeeze of lemon and black pepper.

Patate al Forno con Rosmarino & Sale

Oven Roasted Potatoes with Rosemary and Sea Salt

VEGAN, GF

One of my earliest memories of Italy is of my aunt and uncle's local alimentari. These little markets are common throughout Italy even today, and often have a selection of prepared foods. I seek them out when I visit a new town because they're a fantastic window into an area's products and sources of pride; you might find eggplant caponata in Sicily, or a grilled calamari salad along the coast.

One dish I remember from way back when I was a curious American kid in Sabaudia was simple and familiar: salty roasted sliced potatoes, which can be found just about anywhere in Italy these days.

This preparation makes slices that are a bit thicker and toothier than chips, and when roasted they caramelize around the edges thanks to a dose of quality olive oil. You can slice them by hand with a sharp knife, but if you have a mandoline, it goes a long way to ensuring consistency and an even bake. If you like your potatoes a bit crispier, go for a thinner slice and add 2 or 3 minutes to the bake time, but keep an eye out so you don't burn them.

Rosemary and sea salt are classic, but you can get creative with flavors, too. Toss in some chili powder or paprika for a kick, or swap out the rosemary for herbs like thyme or marjoram, sprinkle with some grated cheese and lemon, or even sprinkle with lavender and drizzle with honey.

Makes 6 to 8 servings

1¾ pounds (800 g) potatoes (russet or red), washed and thinly sliced (with a mandoline, if available)

1 to 2 cloves garlic, thinly sliced

Extra-virgin olive oil, q.b.

1 teaspoon (3 g) rosemary needles

Sea salt, q.b.

Preheat the oven to 400°F / 205°C and line a sheet pan with Silpat or parchment.

In a large bowl, soak the potatoes in cold water for about 15 minutes, then drain, dry with a paper towel, and dry the bowl. Place the potatoes and garlic back in the bowl and toss with olive oil until evenly coated.

Spread the potato slices and garlic on the pan, ensuring there's just enough space so that they don't overlap—you want to give their edges room to caramelize. Sprinkle with the rosemary and salt, then bake for about 30 minutes, until golden brown and crisp.

These are spectacular still warm, but are also delicious at room temperature, so it's a great dish to make ahead of time. Just remember, they're *not* potato chips, so I would advise avoiding a bowl as a serving vessel. Lay the slices out on a cutting board or platter with re-usable toothpicks or small forks, as piling them up can make them soggy and compromise all that delicious caramelized goodness.

Bocconcini di Pollo con Salsa Garibaldi
Chicken Nuggets with Garibaldi Sauce

Bocconcini, or "little bites," applies to a number of different foods (most commonly in the U.S. they are small balls of mozzarella cheese), but bocconcini di pollo are essentially Italian chicken nuggets, and are super common at street food stands all over Italy.

As an American, I was so happy to find one of my favorite comfort foods abroad, but I felt they needed a dipping sauce. I came up with this one while I was studying Italian history at Istituto Lorenzo de' Medici in Florence; I learned that although the French have long been credited with duck à l'orange, any Italian will tell you that the famous dish *actually* has origins in Tuscany (where it is called *anatra all'arancia*). I thought it'd be fun to reimagine the poultry and citrus combo, and the Garibaldi cocktail, already made with orange juice, was a natural source of inspiration (especially given the drink's roots in Italian national pride—see the story on page 218).

So while bocconcini di pollo are found all over Italy, this bright and bittersweet condimento is a personal addition. It's bitter and sweet, aromatic and sticky, and is now something I break out to accompany a number of dishes, including Torte di Risotto (page 158) and Mozzarella in Carrozza al Pesto (page 176), as well as grilled meats and seafood.

Makes 16 to 18 bocconcini

BOCCONCINI

1 large egg

1 tablespoon (15 mL) whole milk

Kosher salt, q.b.

Fresh-cracked black pepper, q.b.

¾ cup (90 g) fresh or dried breadcrumbs

½ cup (50 g) grated Parmigiano Reggiano

1 pound (450 g) chicken breasts, cut into bite-sized pieces

SALSA GARIBALDI

Extra-virgin olive oil, q.b.

1 medium shallot, diced

2 large cloves garlic, minced

⅔ cup (150 mL) Campari

1 cup (250 mL) orange juice

½ cup (125 mL) apple cider vinegar

3 tablespoons (60 mL) honey

2 oranges, zest grated, oranges peeled and segmented

Kosher salt, q.b.

Fresh-cracked black pepper, q.b.

MAKE THE BOCCONCINI

Preheat the oven to 350°F / 175°C and line a sheet pan with Silpat or parchment.

Prepare a breading station: In one dish, beat the egg with the milk, salt, and pepper. In a second dish, combine the breadcrumbs and grated cheese. Dredge the chicken pieces first in the egg mixture, then the breadcrumbs, and arrange on the lined sheet pan, leaving space between.

Bake for 12 to 15 minutes, flipping halfway through, until golden brown and crisp. Alternatively, fry the nuggets in oil heated in a large nonstick pan, and drain on a paper towel.

MAKE THE SALSA GARIBALDI

Meanwhile, in a medium saucepan, heat olive oil over medium heat. Add the shallot and garlic and sweat until translucent. Add the Campari and simmer for 2 to 3 minutes. Add the orange juice, vinegar, and honey and continue to simmer until reduced by about one-third. Remove from the heat and stir in the orange zest and segments. Season with salt and pepper to taste.

Serve the hot bocconcini with the Garibaldi sauce.

note The bitterness of this sauce is governed in part by the oranges. At times, I've adjusted the honey up or down to balance with some sweetness, so be sure to taste as you go.

Olive al Forno
Oven Roasted Olives

VEGAN, GF

At the markets in Italy, the sheer variety of olives to purchase by the *etto* (hectogram, or 100 grams) is overwhelming in the best possible way. I personally always like to have a stash to snack on, blend into tapenade, or toss into pasta. Regardless of what kind of briny olives you love most, they get a boost from citrus and herbs in this recipe and are easily adaptable to your flavor preferences and what you have on hand.

While they're one of the most iconic aperitivo snacks and a classic stuzzichino, baked olives are welcome on almost any table, at any meal—eat them warm, room temperature, or out of the fridge the next day.

You can easily double (or triple, or quadruple) the recipe.

Makes 6 to 8 servings

2 cups (about ¾ pound or 350 g) mixed olives (preferably Castelvetrano, Taggiasche or Niçoise, and Picholine)

2 large cloves garlic, sliced

½ cup (125 mL) extra-virgin olive oil

Fresh thyme sprigs, q.b.

Fresh rosemary sprigs, q.b.

Strips of zest of 1 orange or 1 lemon (or a combination)

1 teaspoon (3 g) red pepper flakes (optional)

Kosher salt, q.b.

Preheat the oven to 525°F / 275°C and spray a baking dish with nonstick spray.

In a large mixing bowl, combine the olives, garlic, oil, herbs, citrus zest, and pepper flakes, if using, and season with salt. Spread the olives in the baking dish and roast for 10 to 12 minutes, until fragrant; the oil should sizzle a bit and the garlic will be browned. Serve warm or at room temperature.

note These are also fantastic with a little brown sugar and cinnamon, which makes for a sweet/salty/spicy contrast that's absurdly crave-able. To try, toss the olives with ½ teaspoon (2 g) ground cinnamon and 2 to 3 teaspoons (5 g) brown sugar while still hot from the oven. I can't say enough about how much I love them like this.

Spiedini di Maiale & Datteri alle Erbe
Pork and Date Herb Skewers with Spiced Orange Glaze

Dates are native to the Middle East and North Africa, but thanks to globalization and migration they have worked their way onto the Italian table in a major way. Southern regions rely on dates to bring sweetness and texture to many dishes, and Sicily has begun to cultivate date palms. While these sweet fruits are frequently featured in dessert and pastry, sometimes stuffed with whipped mascarpone or in chocolate panforte, they make an ideal complement and counterpoint to roasted meats with their concentrated, caramelly sweetness and chew.

These skewers make a perfect addition to your stuzzichini spread if you're looking to offer something a bit more substantial, and the sweet-savory balance—plus the addition of bread to make a sort of crouton that absorbs so much of that delicious pork flavor—is sure to keep things interesting.

The spiedini are fantastic with a simple drizzle of good-quality extra-virgin olive oil and a squeeze of lemon, or you can pair with some of the other sauces in this book: The Cherry Mostarda (page 184), Strega Citrus Vinaigrette (page 186), and Salsa Garibaldi (page 78) all play well with both the pork and the dates. I like to serve them still on the skewers, which makes them ideal aperitivo food, but you can always slide them off and create more of a plated presentation, or lay a few over a bed of arugula as a salad.

Makes 6 to 8 small skewers or 14 to 16 toothpick-sized servings

1 to 1¼ pounds (about 500 g) pork tenderloin or lamb loin, trimmed and cut into bite-sized (1-inch) cubes

Kosher salt, q.b.

Fresh-cracked black pepper, q.b.

Needles from 1 sprig fresh rosemary, chopped

5 fresh sage leaves, chopped

1 large clove garlic, minced

2 tablespoons (30 mL) extra-virgin olive oil

12 dates (about 1 cup), pitted and halved

Stale bread, cubed

Heat the grill to medium. If using wooden toothpicks as skewers, soak in water for 30 minutes to prevent burning and drain.

Season the pork with salt and pepper. Combine the herbs, garlic, and oil in a large bowl, then toss the pork in the mixture until well coated. Thread each skewer with a date, a pork cube, and bread to your liking. Grill for 5 to 8 minutes, turning once, until the pork is cooked through.

Cavoletti di Bruxelles & Pancetta Spiedini con Glassa Balsamica Dolce & Piccante
Brussels Sprout and Pancetta Skewers with Sweet and Spicy Balsamic Glaze

GF

This spiedini was inspired by the combination of Brussels sprouts and bacon I always loved when it showed up on my family's Thanksgiving table in the States. In this case, pancetta gives it an Italian spin.

Balsamic Glaze is one of those condiments that has so much going on and is so satisfying, balanced, and diverse that it's hard to imagine not finding a spot for it on the table at every meal. Here, the way it marries the mild bitterness of grilled Brussels sprouts with salty pancetta and a kick of red pepper is a masterful manipulation of flavors.

Makes 6 to 8 small skewers

5 to 6 cups (about 1 pound or 450 g) Brussels sprouts

1 to 1¼ cups (225 to 250 g) pancetta cubes

Balsamic Glaze (recipe follows)

Heat the grill to medium. Wash the sprouts and dry them with a paper towel.

Bring a large pot of water to a boil, then simmer the sprouts for about 5 minutes, until tender. Drain and cool, then compose the skewers, alternating sprouts and meat.

Grill for about 2 minutes per side, until slightly charred and crispy. Drizzle with the glaze and serve.

note Pancetta cubes come in a variety of sizes. If yours are on the smaller side (¼-inch pieces or smaller), the meat may burn on the grill while the sprouts are cooking. So you'll want to sauté the meat first on the stovetop until crispy, then set aside. Grill the skewered sprouts alone, then add the pancetta to the skewers to serve.

BALSAMIC GLAZE

Balsamic vinegar

Honey

Red pepper flakes

Balsamic glaze ratios range widely, and are based in part on how long you plan to simmer the vinegar into a reduction, which can require some time and babysitting! A quick recipe is about 1 cup (250g) balsamic and 1 tablespoon (20 g) honey, simmered for about 10 minutes or until thick enough to coat the back of a spoon. For a kick, combine about 1 teaspoon (3 g) red pepper flakes with the vinegar at the beginning of the simmer, or if you have access to chili-infused honey, you can use that instead.

Spiedini di Pomodoro Fragola Basilico
Tomato and Strawberry Basil Skewers

 VEGETARIAN, GF

A chef friend once explained to me that strawberry and tomato are nearly interchangeable in recipes (a detail that launched a thousand strawberry pasta sauce experiments), but that they are also fantastic together, and can always be joined through fresh herbs and some kind of creamy fat. In this case, mozzarella and basil make the marriage between the two, but their union would also work with mint and burrata, sage and ricotta, rosemary and feta—it's totally up to you.

Use this framework and substitute peaches, cantaloupe, watermelon, or just about any other fruit that happens to be in season, and if skewers are inconvenient or you want to scale up, it also makes for a beautiful salad.

It's fun to eat these skewers one piece at a time, but to get the full effect of this flavor combo, make sure the pieces of each component (tomato, cheese, strawberry) are small enough to pop into your mouth in a single bite.

Makes 6 skewers

6 fresh strawberries, halved if needed

6 cherry tomatoes

6 mozzarella bocconcini, ciliegine, or pearls (these are slightly different sizes but all small balls of cheese will work)

Fresh basil leaves, q.b.

Balsamic vinegar or a simple vinaigrette, for drizzling

Kosher salt, q.b.

Fresh-cracked black pepper, q.b.

Wash the strawberries and tomatoes, removing the tops from both. Cut the strawberries, tomatoes, and mozzarella into pieces, if you like.

Thread the strawberries, cheese, and tomatoes onto the skewers with basil leaves in between. Serve with a drizzle of balsamic vinegar or a vinaigrette, a sprinkle of salt, and a few twists of black pepper.

Spiedini di Gamberi al Pesto Rosso
Red Pesto Shrimp Skewers

 GF

Until I visited Sicily for the first time, I didn't realize pesto could be anything other than the bright green, basil-based paste my grandmother made for her pasta. Then, at a small trattoria on the side of the highway, I tried the Trapanese-style sauce that was served with busiate pasta (a flat, corkscrewed long noodle) and the island's famed *gamberi rossi* (red shrimp), and thus began my initiation into a whole class of delicious, versatile condimenti.

In this version, roasted red peppers bring a subtle sweetness to red pesto. It's a wonderful complement to grilled shrimp and a fun change of pace from your typical jarred cocktail sauce, but it's also endlessly useful in other ways: Spread it on toast, toss with pasta, or smear on a plate under a pile of roasted cauliflower and top with pickled raisins. Il cielo is the limit.

Makes about 3 cups pesto rosso

1¾ cups (100 g) sun-dried tomatoes, drained and chopped

⅔ cup (100 g) roasted red peppers, drained and chopped

⅓ cup (40 g) grated Parmigiano Reggiano

1 large clove garlic, peeled

¼ cup (35 g) almonds, toasted

3 tablespoons (45 mL) extra-virgin olive oil

Kosher salt, q.b.

Fresh-cracked black pepper, q.b.

Shrimp, prepared as desired

Combine the tomatoes and peppers in a food processor and blend until you have a homogenous mixture. Add the cheese, garlic, and nuts and continue to blend until creamy, drizzling in the olive oil. Season with salt and pepper. You can also make the pesto by hand, using a sharp knife to chop the tomatoes and peppers, then combining them with the remaining ingredients in a medium mixing bowl. The result will be a bit less creamy and more rustic. Store any leftover pesto in an airtight container for up to a week in the refrigerator.

Serve the pesto with shrimp in your preparation of choice—grilled on skewers or steamed and chilled both work beautifully. You can spoon the pesto over the shrimp, serve on the side as a dip, or for a bit more visual flair, smear on a plate and lay the skewers on top.

Pomodori Marinati
Marinated Tomatoes

 VEGAN, GF

These simple marinated tomatoes are like little gemstones, bursting with bright, classic flavors and unexpectedly ideal for aperitivo snacking. I associate them with fond memories of my grandfather's garden and my grandmother's table, as well as little bowls on the table at a piazza bar in the summertime, when they appear alongside cocktails with toothpicks and toasted bread.

In that style, you can serve these straight, pile them on top of Fett'unta (page 111), or use them as a garnish for anything from Crostini de Baccalà Mantecato (page 125) to Torte di Risotto (page 158). They're fantastic in a salad, tossed with grilled in-season corn cut straight from the cob and combined with fresh basil, or with sliced avocado and a squeeze of lime juice. I even love to serve them with crispy, salty potato chips. You can also feature them in a more substantial setting, as a side dish for a flank steak or tossed into a light and summery pasta and buried in grated Parmigiano.

Makes about 4 servings

18 to 20 cherry tomatoes, halved

Kosher salt, q.b.

3 tablespoons (45 mL) balsamic vinegar

1 small red onion, peeled and sliced

2 large cloves garlic, sliced

Pinch red pepper flakes (optional)

½ cup (125 mL) extra-virgin olive oil

Toss the tomatoes with salt and the vinegar. Add the onion, garlic, pepper flakes if using, and oil, and toss to coat well. Marinate in the refrigerator for at least 30 minutes, or more if you have time! Store in the refrigerator in an airtight container for up to one week.

Lecca Lecca al Parmigiano
Parmigiano Lollipops

 VEGETARIAN, GF

At the start of an event to introduce a group of journalists to the culture and culinary treasures of the Collio area of northern Italy, we were greeted with this whimsical bite. To see lollipops—or *lecca lecca* in Italian—on the menu was unexpected, given the professional nature of the gathering, but they made more of an impression than any of the courses that followed. Our hosts were thrilled to hand us something so simple to pair with our cocktails, so evocative of childlike enjoyment yet sophisticated in flavor and representative of Italian cuisine.

This recipe could hardly be simpler—and in fact, I hesitate to call it a "recipe" at all. Yet each time I set these lollipops on a table for guests, I revel in the way people light up with delight and surprise. They are fun and playful, beautiful when bunched up and served in a bouquet and, most importantly, utterly delicious.

The one-ingredient base is also endlessly versatile. You can sub Pecorino Romano for the Parmigiano Reggiano, season with a flurry of fresh black pepper, and call it a Cacio e Pepe Pop. Add poppy or sesame seeds, or spices like pepper flakes, cumin, coriander, turmeric, or even za'atar. I love to blend in a bit of freeze-dried fruit powder like strawberry or raspberry for a sweet and savory spin that's also visually stunning. For a simple fruity addition that is a literal "spin" on spaghetti al limone, dust with freshly grated lemon zest as soon as you remove the tray from the oven.

You can even forgo the stick if you prefer straight cheese crisps, which are a great textural addition to anything from salads to egg sandwiches to pizza as a topping.

Makes 6 lollipops

About 1 cup (about 100 g) grated Parmigiano Reggiano

6 wooden sticks (skewers or popsicle sticks)

Red pepper flakes, q.b., optional

Seeds like poppy or sesame, q.b., optional

Preheat the oven to 425°F / 220°C and line a sheet pan with Silpat or parchment.

Make rounds of grated cheese on the paper (about 15 g each), leaving space in between. You can also use a biscuit cutter or similar as a guide if you want more precise rounds, but try to spread as evenly as possible so baking is consistent. Lay a stick in each circle, with one end of the stick reaching to the center. Sprinkle more cheese to cover the stick, then bake for 5 to 6 minutes, until golden brown.

Remove from the oven and allow to cool completely; they will still be pliable while warm. Use a thin spatula to carefully lift up the lollipops, then serve in a basket, or stick them into another treat as a garnish. Serve with sprinklings of red pepper or poppy or sesame seeds if you like.

Cipolline Agrodolce
Sweet and Sour Onions

 VEGETARIAN, GF

In American culture, the idea of an onion as a snack probably calls to mind a big yellow bag of Funyuns, or something in the fried category (of the rings or "bloomin'" varieties). In Italy, while sometimes served as a *contorno* (a side dish) to steak or pork, these bite-sized alliums make an ideal stuzzichino and cocktail partner, too. The counterplay between the sticky, sweet-sour syrupy cipolline and a palate-scrubbing, bitter spritz is perfect. One bite, and I'm certain you'll find yourself popping onions instead of cheese puffs in no time.

Some optional additions: Sprinkle the onions with fresh herbs such as thyme, oregano, chives, marjoram. Or add dried fruit like raisins or dates when just a few minutes are left in the simmer. And seeds (sesame or poppy) or crushed nuts provide a great pop of texture that can be tossed into the finished onions.

Makes 6 to 8 servings

1½ to 1¾ pounds (650 to 800 g) cipolline or pearl onions, washed

3 tablespoons (45 g) unsalted butter

¼ cup (50 g) packed brown sugar

Kosher salt, q.b.

Fresh-cracked black pepper, q.b.

¼ cup (60 mL) balsamic or other vinegar (white wine or apple cider works well)

1½ cups (350 mL) water, room temperature

Blanch and peel the onions: Bring a large pot of water to a boil, and prepare an ice bath. Trim off the root end of each onion, then boil for 30 to 60 seconds. Strain and transfer to an ice bath. At this point, the onions should be easy to squeeze out of their skins.

Melt the butter in a medium saucepan over medium heat, then add the sugar. Cook until the sugar dissolves, about 3 minutes. Add the onions and season with salt and pepper. Increase the heat slightly and add the vinegar and water. Simmer for 25 to 30 minutes, until the liquid has mostly evaporated and the onions are tender.

Remove from the heat and serve, hot or at room temperature, with toothpicks.

Verdure Sottaceto
Pickled Vegetables

 VEGAN, GF

As an aperitivo snack, crunchy, vinegary veggies are a great contrast between sips. The acid also makes for an ideal palate cleanser for fattier dishes like fritti or rich cheeses, and the vegetables pair beautifully with lots of bitter drinks. Sometimes I like to serve these as a mixture; other times I prefer to choose one or two vegetables for a specific purpose, or as part of a designed menu. Either way, I try to keep in mind the original intention of pickling vegetables—to highlight and preserve a special piece of in-season produce so spectacular, compelling, and precious that it is worth the extra process, so that the vegetables can be marveled at and enjoyed anytime. To me, that's a little bit of magic no matter how you serve it.

Makes 6 to 8 servings

1 pound (450 g) vegetables (cauliflower, carrots, green beans, fennel—lots of options!)

4 large cloves garlic, peeled

2 to 3 sprigs fresh herbs (rosemary, thyme, marjoram), optional

Spices (mustard seed, anise seed, cloves, coriander), q.b., optional

1 cup (250 mL) water, room temperature

1 cup (250 mL) vinegar (cider, rice, red or white wine, balsamic)

1 to 1½ tablespoons (8 to 12 g) kosher salt

Wash the vegetables and cut them into preferred shapes and sizes. Soak in salted water for about 1 hour. Drain and divide into preferred containers, leaving about ½ inch of headspace. Wide-mouth glass jars work well here; the yield will depend on which vegetables you choose but this recipe should work with one or two pint jars. Divide the garlic and herbs and spices (if using) between the containers.

In a saucepan, bring the water, vinegar, and salt to a boil. Reduce the heat and simmer until the salt is dissolved. Pour the pickling liquid into the jars over the vegetables and allow to cool to room temperature. Seal and store in the refrigerator.

These are tangy and tasty right away, but for a more developed pickled flavor, wait at least 48 hours to produce the best results. Since this quick pickle method doesn't include a stabilizing canning process, the veggies will need to be refrigerated, but can last up to 2 months.

note This produces a pretty crunchy pickle; if you prefer softer vegetables, boil them for a few minutes and drain before packing into jars.

Frutta Sottaceto
Pickled Fruits

VEGETARIAN, GF

Like their veggie cousins, pickled fruits are briny and captivating, but sweet, too, maintaining much of their original personality while reflecting the spices and flavors of the pickling liquid. Also very snackable on their own, pickled fruits can make a great substitute for classic jams and marmalades on a cheese plate, garnish a cocktail, or be spooned over gelato for dessert.

I tend to use whatever is in season, but some of my favorite pickling fruits are raisins, kumquats, watermelon rind, cherries, and peaches. When I finish the jar, I like to turn the remaining vinegar into a dressing—just sub it in for the vinegar portion of your favorite vinaigrette!

Makes 6 to 8 servings

1 pound (450 g) fruit (berries, apples, pears, kumquats, raisins, and even watermelon rind all work well)

Spices (whole cloves, cinnamon sticks, fennel or anise seed, fresh ginger root all work well), q.b., optional

1 cup (250 mL) water, room temperature

1 cup (250 mL) vinegar (cider, rice, red or white wine, balsamic)

1 tablespoon (20 mL) honey

1 to 1½ tablespoons (8 to 12 g) kosher salt

Wash the fruit and cut into preferred shapes and sizes. Divide into preferred containers, leaving about ½ inch of headspace. Wide-mouth glass jars work well here; the yield will depend on which fruits you choose but this recipe should work with one or two pint jars. Divide the spices, if using, between the containers.

In a saucepan, bring the water, vinegar, honey, and salt to a boil. Reduce the heat and simmer until the salt is dissolved.

Pour the pickling liquid into the jars over the fruit and allow to cool to room temperature. Seal and store in the refrigerator.

These are tangy and tasty right away, but for a more developed pickled flavor, wait at least 48 hours to produce the best results. Since this quick pickle method doesn't include a stabilizing canning process, the fruits will need to be refrigerated, but can last up to 2 months.

4

CROSTONE, PANE & PANINI
Toasts, Breads, and Sandwiches

Bread is a fundamental part of the stuzzichini ritual, so many of these bites are composed atop slices of it or coated in crumbs of it and deep fried, drawing on a range of carbohydrate customs and capabilities.

A Peninsula of Pane

Pane can mean hundreds of things throughout Italy's twenty regions, so to understand the story of Italian bread, let's take a little *giro* (tour) for a brief introduction to each area's proudest contributions to the carbohydrate canon.

BABA RUSTICO, from Campania

I've heard baba rustico referred to as a "soft, salty doughnut," which is to say, I was immediately sold. As a very classic Neapolitan preparation, the real thing is more of a Bundt cake than what an American might call a doughnut, but the saltiness is no joke. That's thanks to a heavy dosing of cured meats—usually in an array of prosciutto, salami, or whatever is on hand—as well as hunks of cheese, which could be anything from provolone or scamorza to grated Grana Padano or similar. This bread is yeasted and egg-enriched and could be a meal all its own, but is also perfect as part of an aperitivo paired with cocktails and conversation.

BRIOCHE COL TUPPO, from Sicily

Sicilians are quite proud of their *sfincione*—a focaccia-style bread similar to that of Liguria—and with good reason. But for me, the brioche col tuppo tops the list of must-haves when hanging out on the island. Maybe that's because this particular loaf, which has a "hat" baked on top (hence the name, *col tuppo*, a nod to the dialect word for a popular women's hairstyle), is most often used as a vessel for eating gelato or granita. That said, the sweet, buttery roll also makes perfect sandwich bread, and is delicious when toasted and smeared with more butter, and/or stuffed with cured meats, fresh slices of Sicilian tomato, and local cheeses.

BUCCELLATO DI LUCCA and PANE ALTOPASCIO, from Tuscany

Pane Toscana is the most common bread associated with this central region, but Tuscany does a lot more than the saltless namesake when it comes to carbs. Find buccellato di Lucca, a brown bread with raisins and anise seeds that comes in both ring and loaf forms. Or pane Altopascio, a dark bread that is yeast-free, allowing the flavor of whole grains to take center stage.

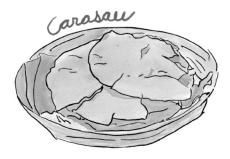

CARASAU, from Sardinia

Also known as "parchment bread" for its wispiness, or "music paper bread" because of the crunch it makes when breaking into it, Sardegnan carasau is an ideal aperitivo staple. This product of yeast, flour, salt, and water is paper thin, somewhere between a cracker and a flatbread. It's ideally suited for toppings of meats, cheeses, and spreads, but is also very satisfying as a crispy snack all on its own.

CRESCIA, from Marche

In Marche, crescia is often referred to as "Easter cheese bread," because it is made with cheese, and typically consumed around Easter. Easy enough, right? Wrong. Like so many things in Italian cuisine, it can vary wildly: from almost as thin as a pancake and called *crescia sfogliata*, which is more of a crisp and flaky flatbread, to a towering, domed loaf. The latter, meant to relieve the diner of their obligatory abstinences during Lent, is a rich treat enriched with plenty of egg and sometimes laden with pricey, indulgent ingredients like black pepper (once considered a luxury item), lardo or other meats, and pecorino or other cheeses. Even sweet versions exist, opulent with cinnamon or hazelnuts, cocoa or vanilla.

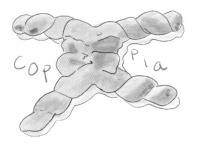

COPPIA FERRARESE, from Emilia-Romagna

The coppia Ferrarese goes by many names, including ciopa and ciupeta, but its appearance is singular and befitting those terms. It is composed of two strips of dough, joined in the center as a "couple" (*coppia*). Allegedly the bread was created to resemble the hip and curly sixteenth-century hairstyle of Lucrezia Borgia (wife of Duke Alfonso d'Este). This fashionable bread obtained PGI status in 2004 and is made with flour, malt, olive oil, and lard.

FOCACCIA, from Liguria

One of the more well-traveled Italian bread staples comes from the third-smallest region of Italy, Liguria. But while the image of an oily, spongy bread topped with sea salt and rosemary needles is very much the most iconic version, the cloudless blue Ligurian sky is the limit for how it can be adapted and tweaked. Some focaccia are topped with grapes during harvest or studded with olives. Others are stuffed with cheese. They can be fluffy and tall or thin or even crispy. Focaccia salata is classic as part of an aperitivo, but sweet versions exist as well; it's not even entirely unusual to find it treated like biscotti and dunked in a cappuccino at *colazione* (breakfast).

FRISELLE, from Puglia

Friselle is a crunchy, round bread product that has made a name for itself far beyond the peninsula's borders. It usually looks like a bagel but behaves more like a cracker. A classic preparation is to top it simply with in-season tomatoes tossed with olive oil and thyme—as a rustic bruschetta—but it is often traditionally soaked with seawater first to soften. This charming preparation is known as *bagnare le friselle*—which essentially translates into English as "bathing bread."

FUGASSA, PANDORO, from Veneto

Veneto is famous for a number of sweet breads, particularly associated with holiday celebrations. Fugassa or fugassin, an egg-enriched dough with honey and lots of butter, is a classic Easter treat. More well known is the pandoro (or *pan d'oro*, meaning "golden bread"), a close relative of panettone; it is set apart by the star-shaped mold used to create its distinctive shape.

Fugassa

GRISSINI, from Piemonte

Piemonte has gifted the world the classic grissini, which can be found not only all over Italy, but in bread baskets and on bartops all over the world. The crispy long sticks are iconic, addictive, and ideal for aperitivo. In this area, though, you can also find biove. This is a more classic bread found all over the region but with particular ties to Pavia; it's often tall with a hard crust and an airy interior that makes a great base for bruschette. Or opt for biovone, a larger version of the same loaf that works for a full slice of toast.

MATERA PGI, from Basilicata

Though it may seem quite a basic bread in composition
(yeast, flour, salt, water), this craggy, cone-shaped loaf
is supposedly meant to resemble the Murgia mountains
of this region. The yeast is also particular; the story goes that
it is the by-product of seasonable fruit, like figs and grapes,
fermented in local water. Given that the region is smack
in the middle of Italy's prime wheat-growing area, the grain
itself brings a nutty, sweet flavor when freshly milled. The
finished loaf is a case study: On the surface, the terse
ingredient list seems no different from that of any other bread,
but when each one is thoughtfully selected and unique, the
finished product is full of its own personality.

MICHETTA, from Lombardy

The michetta is a visually stunning bit of breadwork. When baked,
the scoring creates a look that resembles flower petals, hence
the nickname rosetta. Smaller versions are used for sandwich
bread, which the busy Milanese crowds often grab on the go,
stuffed with salame di Milano or similar delicacies.

PAN DE MOLCHE, from Trentino Alto Adige

This bread utilizes the *molche*, Trentino dialect for the
combination of leftover pulp and peels from pressing olives.
In order to repurpose the waste, it is mixed with flour and
water to create this particular style of bread, which has a
distinct seasonality as a result. Flavorwise, pan de molche
has a hint of bitterness from the olive pulp, and historically
raisins and/or sugar may have been added for balance.

PANE DI SENATORE CAPPELLI, from Abruzzo

The first thing that caught my attention about this bread was its name: "bread of senator hair." Of course, in true Italian fashion, this comical moniker is actually named in tribute to a historical figure—Senator Cappelli—the namesake of a brand of organic durum wheat flour. Cappelli's official title was Marquis of Abruzzo Raffaele Cappelli, Senator of the Kingdom of Italy, and while the story of how this brand came to bear his name could fill an entire book of its own, today it is associated with a high-quality grain marketed as being packed with protein and fiber, as well as an assortment of vitamins and minerals. Though the flour claims Puglia as a birthplace, the Abruzzese developed a bread that highlights its particular attributes and is a source of deep pride in the region.

PAN DI SORC, from Friuli Venezia Giulia

Sorc refers to the maize used in the creation of this classic Friuli bread from Udine. Given its complexity and the abundance of pricey ingredients like sultanas, wild fennel seeds, dried figs, walnuts, and cinnamon—not to mention three different grains (wheat, rye, and corn)—the loaf is unsurprisingly linked to times of celebration, particularly Christmas. Pan di sorc has a distinctly alpine flair, and though it's sweet and delicious on its own, it's perfect paired with local meats and cheeses, too.

PAN NOCIATO and TORTA AL TESTO, from Umbria

Pan nociato (fresh bread) of Umbria comes in interesting variations. While characterized by raisins, pecorino, and walnuts, these additions are at times mixed directly into the dough and distributed throughout (which can result in nearly purple slices), or, at others, stuffed inside and made into a handheld roll that looks more like a dumpling. Torta al Testo, on the other hand, is an unleavened flatbread typically stuffed with meats and cheeses, and more closely resembles a pita.

PGI GENZANO CIRIOLA, from Lazio

Lazio has more to offer than Roman pastas, and when it comes to bread, the region maintains its sense of high drama by shaping the Genzano ciriola loaves to resemble flames, as *ciriola* means "candle." Though the bread itself is basic in terms of its composition (salt, yeast, flour, water, and olive oil), the options are endless when crafting a panino stuffed with myriad Lazian specialties. From Veroli, a village in Lazio that my grandmother calls home, there is the ciambella all'anice—a braided, round bread meant to resemble a crown, fragrant with anise seeds.

PITTA CALABRESE, from Calabria

Not to be confused with pita bread, pitta Calabrese, which can be found all over the region, comes in various forms, but perhaps the most iconic of them is a ring-shaped loaf. Pitta can be large format, meant to be sliced and shared, or individually sized and looking more like a bagel. Customization doesn't stop there, though, as this specialty can be found fortified with everything from zucchini flowers to sardines, tomatoes to olives, and of course local specialties like 'nduja and Tropea onions. As such, pitta Calabrese can easily make a self-contained snack or even a meal, and always welcomes creative interpretation.

PIZZA CON I CICCIOLI, from Molise

Like so much of Italy, Molise cuisine is lauded for its resourcefulness—particularly in its bread culture. Both potato and corn versions of a focaccia-style bread exist, utilizing what's available to stretch their ingredients and their dough. But the people of Molise don't skimp on flavor, either. Many breads are flavored with fennel seeds or pepperoncini, all of which are *ottimo* (optimal) when paired with cheeses and meats or mostarde. But then there is the pizza con i ciccioli, a focaccia-like flatbread creation with crispy pork cracklins, making it perfectly tailored for stuzzichini time with a fizzy, bright spritz to wash it all down.

Acciughe con Burro & Limone
Anchovy Toast with Butter and Lemon

It was my birthday when a few tiny fish and a cozy little spot introduced me to the essence of Italian hospitality. Trattoria Marione, located in the heart of Florence's city center, is known for its classic Tuscan cuisine, so naturally, to pair with an on-the-house welcome glass of bubbly, we ordered the very simple *piatto tipico* (classic plate, or traditional dish).

The thing about simplicity is that it leaves nowhere to hide. Every element must be very good, or the whole thing can be very, very bad. But what amazed me even beyond the quality of the ingredients was the abundance, in particular, of the *burro* (butter). Butter is an expensive ingredient and is treated as such throughout Italy, but the layer beneath our anchovies was luscious and thick. It was evident that the restaurant cared about quality, but this spread was also an obvious gesture of generosity and a clear sign that the folks in the kitchen wanted us to feel cared for. It reminded me of my grandmother, who always made sure her guests had the freshest cookies, the biggest bowl of pasta, a pile of her precious imported cheese. It was touching to me, and it was also delicious.

There are hardly any dishes that showcase simple Italian ingenuity and grasp of flavor as well as this one. Salty, savory anchovies; grassy, creamy butter; yeasty, crusty bread; bright, zippy lemon zest.

With just four ingredients, this is adaptable, inexpensive, constantly crave-able, and utterly satisfying. Basta. That said, if you're interested in putting a personal spin on this classic, I'm including a few riffs that I've come up with over the years. And if you're not into anchovies, swap them out for crabmeat (purchased in a can and drained or fresh both work beautifully) or even bay scallops.

Makes about 6 large or 12 small toasts

6 slices sourdough

½ cup (115 g) unsalted butter

8 to 12 anchovy fillets

Grated zest of 1 lemon

Toast the bread and spread the butter on the toast (wall to wall, don't be shy). Arrange the fillets on top, then cut in half if you prefer smaller servings. Sprinkle with lemon zest and serve.

Acciughe con Burro di Arancia Vaniglia
Anchovy Toast with Vanilla Orange Butter

1 whole vanilla bean, or 2 teaspoons
    vanilla extract or vanilla bean paste
½ cup (115 g) unsalted butter, softened to
    room temperature
Grated zest of 1 orange (or your citrus
    of choice; lime and grapefruit work well)
6 slices sourdough
8 to 12 anchovy fillets

If using a vanilla bean, slice it lengthwise and scrape out the seeds using the side of a sharp paring knife. In the bowl of a stand mixer, or in a large mixing bowl using a hand mixer, combine the butter and vanilla seeds (or extract or paste) and whip on a high speed until light and fluffy. Fold in the orange zest (reserve a sprinkle for garnish) and continue whipping on a high speed for another minute or two, until combined. If you don't have a mixer, you can fold by hand—the texture will just be more like spreadable classic butter than the airy whipped version.

Toast the bread and spread the butter on the toast (wall to wall, don't be shy). Arrange the fillets on toasts, then cut in half if you prefer smaller servings. Garnish with the reserved orange zest and serve.

note Use the juice from the orange for a complementary cocktail like the Garibaldi (page 218) or a Virgin Venetian (page 248).

Acciughe con Burro di Cocco Tostato al Miele
Anchovy Toast with Toasted Coconut and Honey Butter

½ cup (115 g) unsalted butter, softened to
    room temperature
¼ cup (80 mL) honey
2 tablespoons (10 g) toasted coconut
    (sweetened or unsweetened both work,
    depending on your taste)
6 slices sourdough
8 to 12 anchovy fillets

In the bowl of a stand mixer, or in a large mixing bowl using a hand mixer, combine the butter and honey and whip on high speed until light and fluffy. Add the toasted coconut (reserve a sprinkle for garnish) and continue whipping on a high speed for another minute or two, until combined. If you don't have a mixer, you can fold by hand—the texture will just be more like spreadable classic butter than the airy whipped version.

Toast the bread and spread the butter on the toast (wall to wall, don't be shy). Arrange the fillets on toasts, then cut in half if you prefer smaller servings. Garnish with reserved toasted coconut and serve.

note Uses for leftover butter beyond anchovies: bake into cookies; spread on toast, pancakes, or muffins at breakfast time; or my personal favorite, dress a pasta. Toasted Coconut and Honey Butter with red pepper flakes and grated Parmigiano Reggiano makes for one unique and delicious tagliatelle sauce, as does Vanilla Orange Butter with creamy ricotta-filled ravioli and a few cracks of black pepper.

Focaccine di Rosmarino & Lardo
Rosemary and Lardo Focaccine

In the U.S., we commonly think of "lard" as an alternative to butter, oil, or shortening, commonly used as a lipid in baking. In that case, the animal fat (typically pork) is rendered, clarified, processed, and packaged—designed to be as neutrally flavored as possible. Lardo, on the other hand, is the same animal fat, but lovingly cured with spices and aged, with the intention of showcasing flavor on its own. In this iteration, lardo is unctuous and indisputably delicious, packed with melt-in-your-mouth flavor.

Here, focaccine are diminutive versions of the olive oil–soaked specialty we know and love. Slices of lardo practically dissolve into the spongy bread, and piney rosemary gives depth to the whole affair, marrying the two components together.

You can use these focaccine for just about anything. Stud with grapes and season with thyme in the fall, top with a poached egg and crispy prosciutto at brunchtime, or enjoy them semplice, with just a drizzle of quality olive oil and a sprinkle of sea salt.

Makes about 4 focaccine (2½ inches)

¼ cup (60 mL) whole milk

¼ cup (60 mL) water, room temperature

1 teaspoon (3 g) active dry yeast

2 teaspoons (15 mL) honey

1⅔ cups (200 g) 00 flour

Kosher salt, q.b.

¼ cup (60 mL) extra-virgin olive oil, plus more for drizzling

3½ to 4 ounces (80 to 100 g) lardo, thinly sliced

Needles from 2 to 3 sprigs fresh rosemary

Flake sea salt, q.b.

Pour the milk and water into a small bowl and mix in the yeast. Add the honey and stir, then set aside until the mixture froths a bit, about 15 minutes.

In a large mixing bowl, sift the flour with salt, then make a well. Add the oil and the yeast solution to the well and mix until you have a homogenous mixture. You can also do this in a stand mixer with a dough hook on a low speed.

Cover the dough and rest for about 10 minutes. Shape into a smooth ball, then cover with a clean towel and allow to rise for 1 to 2 hours.

Preheat the oven to 350°F / 175°C and grease a sheet pan with oil.

Turn the dough onto a lightly floured surface and use a floured rolling pin to roll to about ¼ inch thick. Use biscuit cutters or the top of a pint glass to cut out rounds, then re-roll remaining dough and continue until all the dough is used. Alternatively, separate the dough into pieces, form balls, and gently roll into rounds. This will give you a slightly less uniform result.

Arrange the focaccine on the sheet pan, allowing space in between. Make impressions with your fingers (about four per dough round is typical) and drizzle generously with olive oil. Bake for 18 to 20 minutes, until golden and crisp on top. Lay slices of lardo over the still-hot focaccine. Sprinkle with rosemary and sea salt and serve, or stuff with meats and cheese of your choice—or even PB&J!

Unpacking Lardo's Origins

A fun fact about lardo (the subcutaneous tissue from the dorsal-lumbar region of a pig—also known as its back fat) is that its origins can be traced back to Colonnata in Tuscany, where it was cured in boxes called *conca di marmo* carved from the famous Carrara marble. The marble itself was seasoned with garlic, which added flavor, but also mitigated the porousness of the stone.

Artisans then filled the box about halfway, alternating layers of the fat with herbs and spices (usually rosemary, sage, anise, coriander, and even cinnamon), before flooding the rest with a saltwater solution. This salt-curing slightly dehydrates the fat, and the result resembles a shortening or spreadable butter. It continues to tell a story about resourcefulness, and how one region's raw materials—even the ones that aren't edible—can influence the country's cuisine in unexpected ways.

While the marble boxes aren't quite as common today, it is still possible to find some artisans carrying on this custom, while others have embraced more modern methods. Either way, opening a package of lardo is always a treat.

Fett'unta
Oil-Drizzled Toast

VEGAN

Not long ago, I received a message from a friend visiting Florence. "What's with the bread here?" he asked, and went on to call it "flavorless" and disappointing. Fortunately, I was prepared for this line of questioning, because despite Tuscany's international culinary renown, pane Toscana is notorious for being very *blah*. The reason is that it is one of the rare breads made without salt—arguably one of the most important elements. But as we've seen before, Italian food is rarely without an explanation, and many believe that historically salt was probably just too pricey to be a part of the daily loaf. That said, there's another school of thought that gives the Tuscan people more agency; in this story, pane Toscana is intentionally neutral, so it can act as a stage for the region's famed olive oil (especially the fresh-pressed version released every fall, known as *olio nuovo*). The name for this preparation of pane Toscana is a conflation of *fetta*, or "slice," and *unta*, meaning "oily," and seems to support that theory in its simplicity. If you don't have access to pane Toscana, you can use a classic, salted bread and still appreciate fett'unta.

This recipe is all about method. The grill should be very hot, as the char is as much a part of the flavor profile as any seasoning. Make sure to choose the best oil you can get your hands on, because even with a rub of garlic, when it comes to fett'unta, the oil truly is the main event. That said, it's also a fantastic starting point for a wide world of interpretations. Take it to the West Coast with a California-style fett'unta topped with sliced avocado and Pomodori Marinati (page 87). Drizzle with Balsamic Glaze (page 83) and garnish with chopped fresh mint. Or make it into a deeply satisfying sweet dish by making fett'unta con cioccolato: Just omit the garlic, and while the bread is still hot, lay squares of your favorite dark chocolate on each slice. Allow to melt, sprinkle with flaky sea salt, and enjoy.

Or try my suggested spin on a fett'unta crostini with a chickpea salad in the variation on page 113.

Crusty bread, sliced about ¾ inch thick

Fresh garlic cloves, q.b.

Flake sea salt, q.b.

Fresh-cracked black pepper, q.b.

Extra-virgin olive oil, q.b.

On a hot grill, toast the bread, about 2 minutes each side. The slices should be crisp and slightly charred on the outside, soft on the inside. Rub with garlic cloves to taste while still hot and season with salt and pepper. Drizzle generously with olive oil and serve.

(CONTINUES)

Fett'unta con Ceci di Soia & Acero
Fett'unta with Maple and Soy Chickpeas

Inspired by one of my favorite bites at Babbo in New York City's West Village—a welcome crostini served on the house—this simple chickpea salad is satisfying and substantial when piled on top of crispy bread. Here, I've swapped out the classic balsamic for a maple-soy combo that switches up the Italian flavor profile. If you prefer to keep it classic, though, just omit the maple and soy and add 1 tablespoon balsamic vinegar.

Makes 6 to 8 servings

1 (15-ounce or 425-g) can chickpeas, drained, rinsed, and dried
1 tablespoon (15 mL) extra-virgin olive oil
2 tablespoons (30 g) olive tapenade
1 teaspoon (3 g) red pepper flakes
1½ teaspoons (7 mL) soy sauce
1½ teaspoons (7 mL) maple syrup
Fett'unta (above)

Preheat the oven to 425°F / 220°C and line a sheet pan with Silpat or parchment.

Spread the chickpeas on a sheet pan and drizzle with the olive oil. Toast in the oven for 15 to 20 minutes, until golden brown and slightly crisp.

In a large bowl, toss the still-warm chickpeas with the tapenade, red pepper flakes, soy sauce, and maple syrup. Spoon the chickpea mixture on top of the fett'unta and serve warm or at room temperature. A warning: These little suckers may try to escape, and you can wind up chasing chickpeas all over your plate. If you prefer a spread that doesn't pose a logistical threat, puree the chickpeas using a food processor, or mash with a fork.

note Garlic is omitted here as the fett'unta is already seasoned with some, but if you want to make this a stand-alone salad, add a clove or two (quanto basta), roasted and chopped.

Chickpeas in Italy
A LEGUME LEGACY

Like so many modest products, chickpeas—or *ceci* in Italian—have a history associated with *cucina povera* (literally "poor cuisine") in preparations designed to stretch ingredients, deliver sustaining calories (as they are a nutritionally complete food), and utilize what's available. Today, these humble legumes are prized, put on display as the centerpiece of a dish, and even protected in some cases, like that of the *ceci neri*, black chickpea of Puglia, presided over by the Slow Food consortium.

Grown primarily in central and southern parts of Italy (i.e., warmer climates), ceci are found in innumerable iterations. In the stuzzichini canon, you can find chickpeas fried or baked and crunchy (like the anise-candied chickpeas on page 38), as well as in flour form (in the recipe for Torta di Ceci, page 167). When tossed raw with olive oil, vinegar, garlic, and herbs and piled on crostini, they are a personal favorite. Beyond these local dishes, the influence of Middle Eastern and Grecian culinary traditions on Italian food is evident in the popularity of hummus around the country, which has become a very common aperitivo snack in both bars and in the home.

Bruschette di Barbabietola & Burrata
Beet and Burrata Bruschette

 VEGETARIAN

It could be because they are the color of passion and conveniently shaped like *un cuore* (a heart), but Italians love their beets. Allegedly, Italy is even one of the first areas to intentionally cultivate them, along with Germany, in the mid-1500s. But beets' roots travel back as far as ancient Pompeii, where you will find their likeness decorating the walls of the ancient Lupanar brothel (perhaps early evidence that they're also considered an aphrodisiac).

Prior to living in Italy, I had never associated beets with Italian food. And while they are a staple in the northern regions for specialties like the filled pasta called *casunziei*, the ways in which Italians apply this humble product all over the peninsula are bountiful. If you don't care for the red roots, though, you can substitute carrots, parsnips, turnips, or celeriac here.

Makes 12 to 24 bruschette

½ cup (125 mL) extra-virgin olive oil, plus more for brushing

½ onion or 1 shallot, sliced

1 large clove garlic, sliced

2 to 3 medium beets, cooked and cubed

2 tablespoons (30 mL) balsamic vinegar

1 teaspoon (3 g) red pepper flakes

Kosher salt, q.b.

Fresh-cracked black pepper, q.b.

1 baguette, sliced on a diagonal, no more than ½-inch thick

4 ounces (115 g) burrata, torn into pieces

About ½ cup (10 g) fresh basil leaves

Heat the oil in a medium nonstick pan over medium heat. Add the onion and garlic and sauté until browned and fragrant. Allow to cool to room temperature. In a medium mixing bowl, toss the beets with the vinegar, red pepper flakes, salt, and pepper. Add the onion and garlic and allow to marinate for about an hour.

Preheat the oven to 375°F / 190°C. Brush the baguette slices with oil, place on a sheet pan, and toast in the oven for 10 to 12 minutes, flipping halfway through.

When ready to serve, distribute the burrata and beet mixture evenly among the slices of toast. Garnish with fresh basil. Depending on the size of your slices, you could make 12 to 24 bruschette from this recipe.

Crostone di Sardine con Pesche & Finocchio
Sardine Crostone with Peach and Fennel

There are three bodies of water that lap up on Sicilian shores—and each one of them is home to a bounty of sardines. In the fifteenth century, when the island was under Arab domination, that abundance allegedly inspired a cook named Admiral Euphemius to invent pasta con le sarde to feed his troops. The dish included local fennel, which grows wild in Sicily, and a classic flavor pairing was conceived.

I adore that pasta, and wanted to find a way to incorporate a similar flavor profile into a finger-food format. This crostone is the result of that daydream, and also incorporates peaches for brightness and acidity. The fennel-peach mixture also makes a lovely salad on its own!

Makes 8 servings

1 small fennel bulb, sliced; fronds reserved and minced

1 large clove garlic, smashed

1 tablespoon (15 mL) extra-virgin olive oil

Kosher salt, q.b.

Fresh-cracked black pepper, q.b.

4 slices crusty bread, toasted and halved

2 medium peaches, pitted and sliced

8 ounces (225 g) canned sardines (about 2½ tins), drained and halved

½ medium lemon

Toss the fennel slices and fronds and the garlic with the oil and season with salt and pepper. Arrange the toast on a serving tray and arrange peaches on each slice, then divide the sardines among them. Top with the fennel mixture, squeeze the lemon over each, and serve.

Crostini di Estratto di Pomodoro alle Erbe
Tomato Paste Crostini with Herbs

 VEGETARIAN

One sweltering August, I spent a week on a farm in Sicily through the Anna Tasca Lanza Cooking School, learning all about tomatoes, from how they're sown and grown to the ways they're transformed into various products. To create tomato estratto—or what we commonly call tomato "paste" in the States—we spent days processing, peeling, and pureeing the fresh fruit. We spread the pulp over long, wooden tables and left it to dry in the beating Sicilian sun. Over the course of several days, we took shifts turning the puree with bench scrapers, observing as it gradually thickened, until it had dried to a heady, Mars-red sort of spread, the consistency of a softened, luxurious butter.

To celebrate a job well done, we enjoyed the finished estratto simply spread on toast and sprinkled with Sicilian oregano, flaky salt, and a drizzle of olive oil. It was a revelation.

Of course, most of us don't have the time and resources to make estratto ourselves, but I have found that it's possible to create a delicious approximation, using store-bought tomato paste and various add-ins, that captures the vibrancy and personality of the southern island. The trick is to use a high-quality tomato paste. Seek out a type that comes in a tube rather than a jar, as the former uses salt rather than citric acid to aid in preservation. The citric acid in the jars amps up the tartness of the tomato, while fresh estratto has a highly savory, almost meaty quality; what I've found in tubes comes closer to that quality. Can't find fresh oregano? Basil, mint, or marjoram are also bright complements to the savory tomato.

Sliced baguette

Tomato paste

Fresh oregano leaves

Flake sea salt, q.b.

Red pepper flakes, q.b. (optional)

Extra-virgin olive oil

Toast the bread slightly and allow to cool. Spread the paste evenly on the toasts, 1 to 2 tablespoons for each slice.

Sprinkle with fresh oregano, sea salt, and red pepper if using. Drizzle with oil and serve.

More Toppings for Crostini di Estratto

If you're looking for something a bit more substantial, the following are some potential topping combinations that still capture the spirit of the prized pomodoro:

* Roasted zucchini and mint

* Fried eggplant, raisins, and cinnamon

* Almonds and avocado with crabmeat

* Toasted fennel seed, red pepper flakes, and sliced cucumber

* A fried egg. Basta.

Crostini di Paté di Fave
Fava Bean Pate Crostini

VEGETARIAN

Fava beans are one of those blink-and-you'll-miss-them items available only in the springtime. But if you can get your hands on them, not only are they transcendently delicious but they're also versatile and fun to use. This recipe leans into their seasonality by pairing the beans with fresh mint. But if you can't source favas, you can use chickpeas, green peas, or just about any other legume of your preference.

If you want to customize, you can increase, change, or even omit the herbs. Or dial back some of the oil and punch up the acidity with a squeeze of lemon juice. You can also reserve a handful of whole beans to sprinkle on top of each toast, giving a little textural variation, or garnish with crushed almonds or bits of prosciutto that you quickly crisped in a pan.

Makes 6 to 8 servings

3 cups (550 g) fresh fava beans

2 large cloves garlic, minced

½ cup (125 mL) extra-virgin olive oil

¼ cup (25 g) grated Pecorino Romano

1 teaspoon (3 g) red pepper flakes (optional)

Kosher salt, q.b.

Fresh-cracked black pepper, q.b.

Toasted bread (sourdough, baguette, country loaf, or just about anything you have on hand works)

Fresh mint and/or basil leaves, q.b.

Grated zest of 1 lemon

Blanch the fava beans: Bring a large pot of water to a boil and cook the beans until tender, 3 to 5 minutes. Immediately transfer to ice water for about 1 minute, then drain. Once cooled, shell the beans. You should have 7 to 9 ounces (200 to 250 g) after shelling.

In a food processor, blend the beans with the garlic, drizzling in the oil until pureed. If you don't have a food processor, you can either use a potato masher to create a coarse blend, or simply toss the ingredients together and serve the whole beans as more of a bruschetta-style topping than a spread. Add the cheese and pepper flakes and season the pate with salt and pepper.

Spread the pate on the toasted bread and sprinkle with fresh herbs and lemon zest.

Crostini di Frutta di Stagione, Ricotta & Miele
Crostini with Seasonal Fruit, Ricotta, and Honey

VEGETARIAN

Like so many preparations in this book (and in Italian food in general), it's almost impossible to call this a recipe. Instead, it's an act of trust: You must trust that whatever fruit you choose will pair perfectly with fresh ricotta, good-quality honey, and your choice of crunchy bits and/or herbs and/or spices, as long as it's done with intention and care. You must trust nature, and your intuition.

Some of my favorite seasonal fruits to use include rotund red cherries, juicy figs, buttery pears, and tart peaches, but keep an eye out at the market and an open mind, and I have faith the formula will always deliver.

I use the following as a good starting point per slice: 1 to 2 tablespoons ricotta, 2 teaspoons honey, ¼ cup fruit.

Baguette, sliced on a bias

Extra-virgin olive oil, q.b.

Whole-milk ricotta

Seasonal fruit (cherries, pears, peaches, apples, figs, oranges) cleaned and pitted, cut to your preference

Honey

Nuts, fresh-cracked black pepper, fresh herbs, grated citrus zest, prosciutto (optional)

Brush the baguette slices with oil and toast on a sheet pan in a 375°F / 190°C oven for 10 to 12 minutes. Allow to cool completely.

Spread the ricotta evenly across the slices. Arrange the fruit on each slice and drizzle with honey. Add any optional toppings and serve.

Crostini de Baccalà Mantecato
Salt Cod Crostini

The first time this puree of salt cod was set down in front of me, at a noontime summer aperitivo in the Veneto region of Italy, I didn't expect to like it. In fact, I was hesitant to even try it. But the way my tablemates were talking about it and going back for seconds and thirds inspired me to take a bite. I was hooked. I wondered later if it was just the July breeze and the salty air from the seaside nearby that made me fall in love with this creamy spread, but I've made it enough times at home to know that it holds up no matter the setting.

Traditionally, this dish is made with salt cod, which is then soaked and desalted. But salt cod can be difficult to source, and if you aren't able to find a presoaked version, desalting can take up to forty-eight hours. This recipe uses fresh cod, which is typically sold boneless and skinless in the U.S.

A classic preparation of this Venetian specialty is to serve it on grilled polenta. You can also use the Brown Butter Polenta Crackers (page 32), or simply toasted crostini, as here. You can even stuff the whipped white fish into cherry tomatoes (instead of the tuna salad on page 50), or roasted peppers.

Makes 6 to 8 servings

1 pound (450 g) fresh skinless boneless cod

¾ cup (180 mL) whole milk

½ cup (125 mL) water, room temperature

1 bay leaf

1 large clove garlic, peeled

3 tablespoons (45 mL) extra-virgin olive oil

Kosher salt, q.b.

Fresh-cracked black pepper, q.b.

Toasted bread (sourdough, baguette, country loaf, or just about anything you have on hand works)

Chopped fresh parsley and grated lemon zest, for garnish

Cut the cod into strips. In a large, heavy-bottomed pot, combine the milk and water and bring to a simmer over medium heat. Add the cod, bay leaf, and garlic and cook for 20 to 30 minutes—this varies depending on the size of the fish—or until tender.

Remove the fish from the liquid; skinless boneless cod will come apart during the boiling process, so use a slotted spoon. Discard the bay leaf, but reserve the liquid.

Place the fish and garlic in a stand mixer with a whip attachment and, at a low speed, begin to whip, gradually drizzling in the oil. (You can also do this by hand with a whisk in a medium mixing bowl.) Increase the speed slightly and incorporate a bit of the cooking liquid if needed to get a creamy consistency. Season with salt and pepper.

Spread the baccalà on the toasted bread, garnish with parsley and lemon zest, and serve.

Crostini di Fegatini con Ciliegie Luxardo
Pate Crostini with Luxardo Cherries

In Tuscany, *fegatini* (liver pate, usually chicken) is a frequent guest on many a stuzzichini-laden table. The rich and ultra-savory snack often gets a lift from a drizzle of vinegar or pickled fruit, along with the occasional flurry of crushed pistachios or hazelnuts for texture.

For me, the straight-from-the-jar Luxardo cherries contribute acidity, sweetness, and texture (as the fruit itself is toothsome and referred to as "crunchy" by the Luxardo family). That's to say nothing of flair—a drizzle of the deep garnet cherry syrup is dazzling to both eye and palate.

Makes 4 to 6 servings

PATE

½ pound (225 g) cleaned chicken livers

Extra-virgin olive oil, q.b.

1 medium carrot, chopped

½ medium onion, chopped

½ medium stalk celery, chopped

1 large clove garlic, crushed

¼ cup (60 mL) vin santo (or other sweet white wine)

Fresh sage leaves, q.b.

Fresh rosemary needles, q.b.

2 tablespoons (15 g) capers, chopped

2 anchovy fillets, rinsed

2 tablespoons (30 g) unsalted butter, cold

Kosher salt, q.b.

CROSTINI

Brioche, sliced

Unsalted butter, q.b.

Luxardo cherries, halved; plus syrup from the jar

MAKE THE PATE

Soak the livers in water for about 30 minutes, then pat dry.

In a medium, heavy-bottomed pan, heat 2 to 3 tablespoons oil over medium heat. Add the carrot, onion, celery, and garlic and sauté until softened and the garlic is browned. Add the livers and cook until browned but still pink on the inside, then remove the livers and set aside. Add the vin santo, sage, and rosemary to the pan, cover, and cook on low to reduce the liquid slightly, 4 to 5 minutes.

Remove the pan from the heat and add the livers, capers, anchovies, butter, and salt. At this point you can choose to blend the mixture in a food processor until creamy, or chop with a chef's knife into a more rustic spread. You may have a bit of excess liquid, which you can simply drain off using a mesh sieve, before storing the pate in a jar or other airtight container. Chill the pate in the fridge for at least 1 hour. Store in an airtight container for up to a week in the refrigerator.

PREPARE THE CROSTINI

Before serving, cut the brioche into triangles and toast in a frying pan with butter until crisp. Spread the pate over the toasted triangles and top with cherries, quanto basta (for me, that means two or three per slice, but you can certainly be more generous or more conservative!). Drizzle with additional syrup from the cherry jar.

note Candied orange peel (see page 200) works beautifully instead of cherries. For a more savory (and distinctly luxurious) iteration, serve with grated black or white truffles, if you've got them.

Luxardo

ITALY'S GEM STONE FRUIT

The Luxardo candied cherry—that garnet-colored, syrup-soaked stone fruit of the gods—is produced by a family-run organization with a remarkable history in the Veneto region. But with the cherry's international recognition on the ends of toothpicks and at the bottom of coupe glasses in the best bars on the planet, it's a source of pride for Italians all over.

The exact process of creating that cherry is not something you'll be able to coax from any Luxardo family member, but perhaps the mystery of how simple cherries and sugar can yield such distinctive results is part of what makes its lovers (like me) nearly manic with desire.

During a visit to the Luxardo headquarters during the late spring harvest, Matteo Luxardo, the company's current export director (and fifth generation), walked us through what he referred to as one of their "small" orchards. Here, I made the acquaintance of 600 marasca cherry trees, each of which produces about 100 kilograms of fruit "without steroids." Matteo explained that the pH of the soil is especially well suited to growing the cherries thanks to "former volcanoes" in the area, and that the trees they cultivate begin yielding at five years and continue until they're twenty to twenty-two. In other words, a *lot* of cherries.

That's a good thing, because the candied cherries, which are a slightly larger variety than the ones used to produce Luxardo's famous cherry liqueurs and other products, have to meet an awful lot of demand. The U.S. alone—the company's largest market for the candied fruit—clocks about 2.5 million jars per year. In other words, a river of Manhattans.

The deeply red Luxardo cherries have loyalists, and other established brands like Amarena Fabbri also find a comfortable home on the bartops of cocktail enthusiasts. But today, the market has made room for a range of small batch producers (and even some larger alcohol companies, like Woodford Reserve) who have taken to making their own versions of the famed candied fruit.

Luxardo also makes and distributes jams and other products that are not unfamiliar on aperitivo tables. "We sell a lot of our jams—mainly the apricot, the marasca, and the plum—to restaurants," Matteo said. "They are not so sweet, and go very well especially with fresh cheese, like camembert or ricotta, or even sour yogurt."

And while the classic use of the Luxardo cherry itself may lie at the bottom of a mixed drink, it's right at home in lots of roles. The depths of the sweet-sour flavor, the textural contrast between the crunchiness of the skin and the nearly liquefied flesh—all make the Luxardo cherry a welcome component across the culinary board. It's a natural crowning jewel for a gelato sundae or cheesecake, but also plays balancing roles in savory dishes, from chicken liver to pork chops.

Tramezzini al Burro di Pomodoro
Tomato Butter Finger Sandwiches

VEGETARIAN

At a glance, these little white-bread finger sandwiches might make you nostalgic for a lunch-box PB&J, but the Italian tramezzino is born to be served with an adult beverage. As with any panino, you can use the format for just about anything, and many tramezzini are served with cured meats and cheeses. While tomatoes are often paired with cheese, it is criminal to neglect their affinity for good butter; a little fresh basil gussies up the otherwise totally unfussy preparation.

Makes 6 or 12 small sandwiches

½ cup (115 g) unsalted butter, softened

¼ cup (15 g) sun-dried tomatoes, drained and chopped

6 slices soft white bread, crusts trimmed (reserve to make breadcrumbs)

Chopped fresh basil leaves, q.b.

In a medium bowl, mix together the butter and tomatoes with a rubber spatula until well incorporated. This method yields a rustic spread, but if you'd prefer a creamier finished product, you can also pulse in a food processor until smooth and creamy.

Use the spread to make three sandwiches, adding fresh basil. Cut into triangles and serve.

note Roll the remaining butter mixture in parchment paper into a log and chill in the refrigerator until later use. Tomato butter is delicious on just about everything, from pasta to fish, stirred into a warm bowl of rice or polenta, or even melted and tossed with popcorn.

Piadine con Taleggio & Porcini
Porcini and Taleggio Piadine

VEGETARIAN

A piadina is the Italian answer to tortillas, wraps, naan, flatbread, or whatever you want to call something you can fold or roll up. You can fill them with meats and cheeses, spreads and roasted veggies, even sweet ingredients like honey-whipped ricotta and chocolate—whatever strikes your fancy! You'll find them in the recipe for kebab on page 133, too. But in this example, the prized porcini meets funky Taleggio in a flavor profile common to northern Italian pasta dishes, but in a format far simpler to snack on.

If you can't get your hands on the classic porcini, shiitake, cremini, button, or brown mushrooms work as well.

Makes about six 8-inch piadine

PIADINE

1½ cups (175 g) 00 flour

⅓ cup (75 mL) water, room temperature

1 tablespoon (15 mL) extra-virgin olive oil

1 teaspoon (3 g) kosher salt

PORCINI AND TALEGGIO FILLING

1 pound (450 g) fresh porcini mushrooms

Extra-virgin olive oil, q.b.

Kosher salt, q.b.

Fresh-cracked black pepper, q.b.

2 to 3 sprigs fresh thyme

1¼ cups (10 ounces or 280 g) Taleggio (fontina also works well), sliced

MAKE THE PIADINE

Place the flour in a medium mixing bowl. Gradually add the water and mix well either by hand or using a stand mixer with a dough hook. Add the oil and salt and continue to knead to a pliable dough. Cover and allow the dough to rest for about 30 minutes

Divide the dough into six balls, then rest another 10 minutes. Using a rolling pin, roll the balls into rounds about ⅛ inch thick and 8 to 10 inches in diameter. Pierce the rounds with a fork to prevent puffing during the cooking process.

In a lightly oiled large nonstick pan over medium heat, cook one round until the bottom is golden, 1 to 2 minutes, then flip carefully and cook on opposite side for another 1 to 2 minutes. Stack as you work your way through cooking each piadina. (You can enjoy these with your choice of filling still hot or at room temperature, but I also love to make an abundance of these and freeze for later use.)

Note: You can also make smaller piadine for a snackier version. I find about 4 inches to be a good "fun size."

MAKE THE FILLING

Meanwhile, preheat the oven to 375°F / 190°C and grease a sheet pan with oil or nonstick spray.

Toss the mushrooms with oil, salt, and pepper and arrange on the pan. Strip the leaves from the thyme sprigs and sprinkle among the mushrooms. Roast for about 45 minutes, until the mushrooms are browned and slightly crisp. Drain liquid about two-thirds through the process (reserve the liquid for another use).

ASSEMBLE THE PIADINE

Layer slices of cheese with mushrooms on one half of a piadina and fold over, like a taco. You can present the piadina as a handheld for a more substantial stuzzichino, or cut into smaller sections and serve with a toothpick.

Kebab in Italy

THE REVOLVING, EVOLVING CULTURE OF TURKISH ROTISSERIE

When it comes to Italy, food media tends to focus on nonnas in the kitchen and centuries-old traditions. But the reality is that the country—like most parts of the world—has seen massive changes in its communities as a result of global migration. This has been made evident in the culinary scene, and in many parts of Europe, the prevalence of—and hunger for—doner kebab indicates such a shift.

The doner kebab is of Turkish origin, but this vertical rotisserie (usually a meat mixture that includes beef, lamb, and veal) began its Italian journey by showing up in pizzerie around the country, a seemingly natural extension of grab-and-go, street food–style dining. Today, it's common to find stand-alone *donerie* (doner shops) all over the peninsula, staffed by and filled with not only immigrants, but Italians, too.

And while doner is the most common, there is an entire array of kebab to carve into. "A lot of people in Italy think Turkish kebab restaurants are just for late night food, but really that's only doner kebab," says Ata De Çin, a Turkish-born chef now living in Florence. "There are actually more than thirty-five different types of kebab—shish, fırın kebabı, patlıcan kebabı, adana kebab, güveç kebab, kuzu kebab."

De Çin also explains the history of kebab in his current home, and its audience in Italy. "[Restaurateur] Denis Bertamini opened the first kebab restaurant in Florence in the late 1990s. Now there are about seventy Turkish fast-food restaurants in the city. Even people who mainly eat Italian food love to have a good doner kebab sometimes, especially after they party."

Today, countless born-and-raised Italians have incorporated kebab into routines in the classic form (served on a skewer, or in *yufka*—a traditional Turkish-style flatbread), but there has also been a creative conflation of cultures. You can find kebab pizzas, calzones stuffed with doner meat, and other inspired dishes that truly represent modern Italy's multicultural communities.

It's important to note that this evolution has not always been welcome—kebab shops and vendors have been the target of xenophobia, violence, and even government suppression. But many modern Italians today speak out in favor of a more supportive environment for immigrants, as well as policies that would allow and encourage more businesses to open, serve their communities, and thrive. This kind of cultural exchange, they believe, is part of the true Italian tradition and legacy, and ultimately enriches the country, now and for the future.

The flavors of traditional Turkish doner kebab, with shawarma spices and savory meats, make a natural aperitivo pairing, and these days you're just as likely to find Italians taking their spritz and stuzzichini at a doneria as they are an enoteca. It's also common to find kebab meat rolled up in a typical Italian piadina, and De Çin was kind enough to share his recipe for doner kebab, complete with a garlicky, minty yogurt sauce, which you can find on page 133. It's a delicious representation of modern Italian culture, and further evidence that you can make your aperitivo with any influences that speak to you.

Piadine Doner Kebab con Salsa allo Yogurt

Doner Kebab Piadine with Yogurt Sauce

Chef Ata De Çin says there are a variety of spices common for doner, including paprika, cumin, black pepper, and garlic, and that once the kebab is "wrapped in a piadina like a burrito," it is often served with chickpeas, onions, tomatoes, cabbage, or hot peppers, a side of salad or chips, and a variety of sauces ranging from a traditional spicy chili sauce to ketchup and mayonnaise. For this piadina recipe, he recommends a beautifully creamy, herbaceous, and garlicky yogurt sauce that couldn't be simpler to whip up.

Makes 4 to 6 servings

KEBAB MEAT

1 tablespoon (15 mL) extra-virgin olive oil

1 pound (450 g) ground meat (lamb or beef)

4 large cloves garlic, minced

1 tablespoon (14 g) tomato paste

2 teaspoons (6 g) ground paprika

1½ teaspoons (3 g) ground cumin

1 teaspoon (3 g) fresh-cracked black pepper

SALSA ALLO YOGURT

1 cup (245 g) plain full-fat yogurt

3 large cloves garlic, minced

1 teaspoon (3 g) dried mint

1 teaspoon (3 g) dried oregano

Kosher salt, q.b.

Fresh-cracked black pepper, q.b.

6 piadine (from Piadine con Taleggio & Porcini, page 130)

MAKE THE KEBAB MEAT

Preheat the oven to 400°F / 205°C. Brush the oil on a large sheet of foil.

In a food processor, blend together all the remaining kebab meat ingredients. You can also do this by hand in a large bowl using a rubber spatula.

Turn out the mixture onto the oiled foil, then use your hands to bring the meat together into a large sausage shape. Wrap the foil tightly around the meat mixture, further compressing it into a log. Place the meat in a roasting pan and roast for 35 minutes, or until the internal temperature of the log reads 160°F / 70°C.

Allow the meat to rest for 10 to 15 minutes, then unwrap and thinly slice with a sharp knife.

MAKE THE SALSA ALLO YOGURT

Meanwhile, in a small mixing bowl, combine all the sauce ingredients together using a rubber spatula.

To assemble, layer the doner kebab in the piadine and serve with the yogurt sauce.

Schiacciata di Verdure al Pecorino
Pecorino and Root Vegetable Flatbread

VEGETARIAN, GF

In Tuscany, *schiacciata*—which is pronounced *skee-ah-CHA-tah* and roughly means "crushed," "flattened," or "squashed"—is a versatile word applied to a variety of breads and bread-like things, from a piece of sweet focaccia studded with roasted grapes around the autumn harvest to a savory situation that more closely resembles a panino and comes stuffed with your choice of cured meats and cheeses.

Here, instead of the flour-based, focaccia-like traditional schiacciata, the base is made of blended root vegetables that get a boost from baked-in cheese. There's a slight tang from beets, an earthy sweetness from carrots, and balancing saltiness and chew from pecorino.

They can be served in small bites bursting with flavor on their own or topped with a smear of Mousse di Salmone Affumicato (page 28), a bright swipe of Crema di Piselli (page 65), or a sweet-spicy dollop of Cherry Mostarda (page 184), and make a colorful, gluten-free alternative to classic crostini.

These are great with just about any cocktail, but I especially love them with a Garibaldi (page 218)—the OJ-based drink is a perfect sweet-tart counterpoint.

Makes 6 to 8 servings

1 pound (450 g) beets and carrots (combination and ratio are up to you)

¾ to 1 cup (180 to 250 mL) water, room temperature

1 large egg

2¼ cups (225 g) grated Pecorino Romano or Parmigiano Reggiano

Fresh-cracked black pepper, q.b.

Spices, q.b. (optional)

Preheat the oven to 375°F / 190°C and line a sheet pan with Silpat or parchment.

Wash, peel, and dry the vegetables. Chop and then run through a food processor until well combined and nearly pureed, adding water as needed to facilitate the process. (If your food processor isn't especially powerful, you can facilitate the process by first roasting the chopped vegetables in a 375°F / 190°C oven for about 10 minutes, then pulsing through the food processor until creamy. Don't be tempted to boil first, though, as the additional moisture will make them too wet later in the process.) If you don't have a food processor, you can use the finest side of a box grater for both beets and carrots and then combine; this will result in a slightly more rustic texture.

In a large bowl, mix the pureed or shredded vegetables with the egg and cheese until well combined using a rubber spatula or by hand. Spread on the lined pan into a layer about ¼ inch thick, using a spatula (or smoosh with clean hands). Season to taste. Black pepper is all I reach for most days, but these also work well sprinkled with cumin, cinnamon, caraway seeds, paprika, and red pepper flakes, to name a few.

Bake for about 40 minutes, until browned and slightly crisp. Use a sharp knife or pizza cutter to slice into preferred shapes and sizes. Allow to cool completely, gently remove from sheet pan, and serve. Store in an airtight container in the refrigerator for up to 3 days.

Crostini al Formaggio Liptauer con Ravanello & Erba Cipollina

Liptauer Cheese with Radish and Chive Toasts

VEGETARIAN

The first time someone served me Liptauer cheese was in Friuli Venezia Giulia, a small northeastern region of Italy that bumps up against Austria, Slovenia, and the Adriatic Sea and boasts spectacular views of the peaks of the Dolomite Mountains. When I took a bite, I considered checking a map to see if I was still within the peninsula's borders. Speckled with spicy paprika and decorated with cornichon and radish, it didn't taste like any Italian food I'd ever had. But this is the style of cuisine you'll find in this northern region, where Austro-Hungarian influences still reign supreme. Regardless of where the dish originated, if it ends up in your stuzzichini spread you'll be a happy camper.

Makes 6 to 8 servings

1 cup (225 g) farmer's cheese
(e.g., ricotta, goat, cottage)

2 tablespoons (30 g) chopped
yellow onion

6 anchovy fillets, minced
(or 1 tablespoon or 15 g anchovy
paste)

1 tablespoon (8 g) capers, minced

1 teaspoon (3 g) whole caraway
seeds

1 teaspoon (3 g) ground paprika

Toast points (rye or pumpernickel)

2 to 3 fresh radishes, sliced

Cornichons, q.b.

Chopped fresh chives, for garnish

Combine the cheese, onion, anchovies, capers, caraway, and paprika in a food processor and blend until creamy. You can also do this by hand, resulting in a more rustic spread.

Serve on rye or pumpernickel toast points with radishes and cornichons, and garnish with chives.

note Some recipes call for milk to thin the cheese, or additional spices and flavorings (garlic, mustard powder, chopped pickles). I offer a basic starting point; feel free to make it your own!

Tigelle con Spuma di Mortadella
Flatbreads with Mortadella Mousse

Tigelle are flatbreads that remind me of English muffins, but a touch flatter. Often, you'll find them split open and filled, sometimes with meats or cheeses, other times simply with a spread or spuma. Hailing from the elegant area of Emilia-Romagna, they are often decorated with a design specific to a family or occasion, thanks to a *tigelliera* or *stampo per tigelle*—a special press exclusively designed for tigelle. At home, though, a frying pan will work just fine.

Instead of the spuma di mortadella, try filling the tigelle with hummus, meats, and/or cheeses—your choice! The spuma is also delicious in deviled eggs, or stuffed into squash blossoms and fried.

Makes about 6 tigelle

TIGELLE

⅓ cup (75 mL) water, room temperature

⅓ cup (75 mL) whole milk

1 teaspoon (3 g) active dry yeast

2 cups (240 g) all-purpose flour

1 teaspoon (3 g) kosher salt

1 tablespoon (15 mL) extra-virgin olive oil

SPUMA DI MORTADELLA

⅓ pound (150 g) mortadella

¼ cup (60 g) whole-milk ricotta

¼ cup (25 g) grated Parmigiano Reggiano

¼ cup (60 mL) heavy cream

Kosher salt, q.b.

Pistachios, crushed, q.b.

MAKE THE TIGELLE

In a small bowl, combine the water and milk with the yeast and allow to bloom, about 10 minutes.

In a medium mixing bowl, combine the flour and salt, then mix in the oil. Add the yeast mixture and knead for about 5 minutes, until a dough forms. Rest in the bowl, covered in a warm place, for about 2 hours, until doubled in size.

On a floured surface, roll the dough to about ¼ inch thick. Using a 3-inch biscuit cutter or the top of a floured pint glass, cut out rounds, then re-roll scraps and continue cutting until all the dough has been used. Arrange the rounds on a parchment-lined sheet pan and cover with a clean towel. Proof for another hour in a warm place.

MAKE THE SPUMA DI MORTADELLA

Combine all the ingredients in a food processor and blend until creamy. Garnish with crushed pistachio.

COOK AND ASSEMBLE THE TIGELLE

Heat a nonstick frying pan over medium heat. In batches, cook the tigelle for about 4 minutes on each side. They will puff slightly as they cook. Allow to cool slightly and slice each tigelle in half horizontally. Fill with spuma di mortadella and serve.

Cracker con Acciughe, Cioccolato Fondente & Ricotta
Crackers with Anchovies, Dark Chocolate, and Ricotta

I know, this one sounds weird. But before you throw the small fish out with the seawater, remember that Sicilians created the cannoli, caponata, and—it is sometimes argued—gelato. Each of their creations is a study in texture and a tricky tightrope of flavors. This is a region that deeply understands composition.

I first tasted these crispy bites at an aperitivo in Zafferana Etnea, a commune of Catania situated in the shadow of the mystical Mount Etna. They were paired with a cocktail, featuring a local blood orange amaro and a spray of musky olive oil, that was served with a flaming orange wheel. Needless to say, the whole scene had a flair for the dramatic, but it was this bite that took center stage.

With the salty anchovy and bitter dark chocolate, along with creamy cheese to keep everything in check, what initially seemed like an unusual combination of flavors made complete sense on the palate. These stuzzichini are sweet and salty, crunchy and creamy, with lively pops of citrus and spice, and I found it impossible not to go back for more.

Note: When I say "chocolate," we're not talking about a Hershey bar here. Modica chocolate is dark and bitter, moody and gritty, and has a gripping history all its own (see page 142).

Makes 24 crisps

24 Cracker di Polenta al Burro Bruno (page 32)

1 cup (240 g) whole-milk ricotta

24 anchovy fillets

½ cup (85 g) roughly chopped cioccolato di Modica (or other high-quality dark chocolate)

Grated zest of 1 orange

1 to 2 tablespoons (10 to 20 g) fennel seeds, toasted

1 tablespoon (10 g) red pepper flakes (optional)

In the center of each crisp, spoon ½ tablespoon ricotta. Around the dollop of cheese, wrap 1 anchovy fillet.

Nestle crumbled chocolate into the cheese and top with a dusting of orange zest and toasted fennel seeds. Sprinkle with pepper flakes, if using, and serve.

note You can also use store-bought herbal crackers of your choice, or a simple stoned-wheat cracker, and sprinkle toasted fennel seeds over each finished bite.

The Chocolate of Modica, Sicily

Modica chocolate is made in a particular series of steps, in which the cacao is hand-ground and processed "raw" at around 40°C (just over 100°F). Because of the manual nature of the practice and low temperature, the added sugar doesn't fully melt, resulting in a grittiness and uneven color that characterize the style. The finished chocolate is bitter and a touch astringent, with a pleasantly crunchy texture.

This prized chocolate is not only delicious and unique, but also an edible history lesson. Modica chocolate owes its origin to the Aztecs, who are thought to have invented the practice used in Italy today. When the Spanish conquistadors who had colonized South America later took control of Sicily, it is believed that they transported the process to the island, where it was adopted and evolved into the product we now enjoy.

Today, Modica chocolate adheres to the same centuries-old customs, and is an example of the resistance to industrialization as well as a signifier of the many multicultural influences found in Italian products. So revered is the tradition of Modica chocolate that it is included as a IGP (Indicazione Geografica Protetta) product, which guarantees that any chocolate bearing the Modica moniker is made within a designated area.

Notable modern Modica chocolate producers include Antica Dolceria Bonajuto and Sabadi, and flavors range from traditional dark chocolate, nutmeg, lemon, and pepperoncino to carrot, cola nut, and pomegranate.

Patate Dolci "Crostini" con Mirtilli Tostati & Gorgonzola

Sweet Potato "Crostini" with Roasted Blueberries and Gorgonzola

VEGETARIAN, GF

I first had this take on crostini at an intimate cocktail party, and it wasn't until I took a bite that I realized this was no regular toast (and had to interrupt my conversation to marvel at it: "Did you taste this thing?!"). Perfect for those in your life who require a gluten-free option, or when you're looking for a little spin on the classic base, these bites utilize sliced sweet potato as a stand-in for baguette slices or other sliced carbohydrate, and here are paired with jammy, tart *mirtilli* (blueberries).

Sweet potatoes and blueberries may not be the most common ingredients that come to mind when considering Italian food, but both are fairly abundant around the country. Sweet potatoes fill pastas and even transform into stuzzichini-friendly fries, and blueberries stand out in gelato cases when churned into sorbetto, or when accompanying savory dishes like duck. Their seasons overlap a bit during the months of September, February, and March, but this dish can utilize frozen blueberries as well.

Both ingredients are a natural match for northern Italy's prized Gorgonzola dolce, and with the cheese's striking blue veins this stuzzichino is a perfect cooler weather snack that is deeply delicious and beautiful to behold, and will give you plenty to talk about.

Makes 6 to 8 servings

MIRTILLI TOSTATI

2 cups (340 g) blueberries, fresh or frozen

1 tablespoon (12 g) granulated sugar

6 to 8 fresh sage leaves

PATATE DOLCI

2 large sweet potatoes

Extra-virgin olive oil, q.b.

"CROSTINI"

2 cups (240 g) Gorgonzola dolce

Toasted walnuts, q.b. (optional)

Kosher salt, q.b.

Fresh-cracked black pepper, q.b.

ROAST THE MIRTILLI

If using fresh berries: Preheat the oven to 400°F / 205°C and line a sheet pan with Silpat or parchment. Wash the blueberries and drain. Spread on the lined sheet pan and toss with the sugar and sage by hand. Roast for about 10 minutes, until the berries are bursting. Let cool.

If using frozen berries: Cook in a medium frying pan over medium heat for about 10 minutes, stirring regularly with a rubber spatula, until the liquid reduces and becomes syrupy. You can test this by spooning a bit of the syrup onto a plate and allowing to cool to room temperature to gauge the consistency and thickness.

In either case, allow the blueberries to cool to room temperature and set aside.

(CONTINUES)

ROAST THE PATATE DOLCI

Heat the oven to 425°F / 220°C and grease a sheet pan with nonstick spray or oil.

Cut the sweet potatoes into ¼-inch-thick rounds and toss with the oil. Arrange the rounds on the pan, leaving a bit of space in between. Roast for 15 minutes, then flip and roast for another 10 minutes, until slightly caramelized at the edges and soft in the center. Let cool slightly.

ASSEMBLE THE "CROSTINI"

Top the rounds with Gorgonzola, roasted blueberries, and walnuts (if using). Season with salt and pepper to taste and serve warm or at room temperature.

Pane con Tapenade di Cioccolato
Chocolate Tapenade Toasts

*VEGAN (IF USING VEGAN OR RAW CHOCOLATE)

Maybe you're surprised that this is the second time in this book you've come across dark chocolate in a non-dessert capacity (the first being the Cracker con Acciughe, Cioccolato Fondente & Ricotta on page 141). But once again, Italian resourcefulness is at work, as well as an understanding of an ingredient's capacity beyond what's commonly expected.

Like anchovies, black olives are an assertive flavor, and combined with dark chocolate can make for an intense one-two punch of salt and bitterness. But in this case, a fruity, delicate olive oil works magic in softening both ingredients, brokering a partnership that we may not have seen coming, but can probably all agree (after tasting, of course)—just works.

Makes 6 to 8 servings

1⅔ cups (258 g) black olives, pitted

⅓ cup (56 g) dark chocolate (at least 60% cacao), coarsely chopped

Red pepper flakes, q.b. (optional)

Fresh herbs (like basil, parsley, or sage), q.b. (optional)

½ cup (125 mL) fruity extra-virgin olive oil

Sourdough bread, toasted

Place the olives and chocolate in a blender. Some suggest melting the chocolate first, but I personally prefer a bit more rustic texture to the spread. Add the pepper flakes and the herbs if using. Blend together, gradually adding the oil until you reach the desired consistency. This can also be done by hand or in a mortar and pestle, for a more rustic and less creamy version.

Spread the tapenade on the toasted bread and serve.

Cestini di Pane con Mousse di Broccoli
Bread Baskets with Broccoli Mousse

It was at an elegant aperitivo buffet in Rome that I first encountered these fun bites. You can use a high-quality, home-baked bread to make the happy little edible baskets—or this is also a great opportunity to get creative with a grocery store staple bread loaf. The broccoli mousse is a savory flavor bomb, but you could also use the little cestini for hummus, bruschetta, or just about any filling you can conjure.

Makes 6 servings

CESTINI DI PANE

6 slices soft white bread, crusts trimmed

2 tablespoons (30 g) unsalted butter, melted

MOUSSE DI BROCCOLI

4 cups (about 1 pound or 450 g) chopped broccoli

1 cup (100 g) grated Pecorino Romano

1 large clove garlic, peeled

Kosher salt, q.b.

Fresh-cracked black pepper, q.b.

2 teaspoons (10 to 12 g) anchovy paste (optional)

Red pepper flakes, q.b. (optional)

Fresh basil leaves, q.b.

MAKE THE CESTINI DI PANE

Preheat the oven to 350°F / 175°C and grease a muffin tin with nonstick spray.

Brush the bread slices with the melted butter on both sides. Fit the slices into muffin tin cavities to make cups. Bake for about 15 minutes, until crisp. To remove the cestini from the muffin tin, allow them to cool until you can handle them and tip the tin to release. Unfilled, you can keep these bread baskets in an airtight container in the refrigerator for about 24 hours, but they're best and most crispy when fresh!

MAKE THE MOUSSE DI BROCCOLI

Bring a large pot of water to a boil. Add the broccoli and cook, uncovered, until tender, 5 to 8 minutes depending on the size of the florets. Drain, then combine with the cheese, garlic, salt, and pepper in a food processor. If using, add the anchovy paste and/or pepper flakes. Blend until smooth and creamy. You can also do this by hand with a sharp knife for a more rustic filling.

Divide the broccoli mixture among the bread cestini, garnish with basil, and serve.

note This can be made vegetarian simply by skipping the optional anchovy paste, but if you'd like to maintain that umami punch from the salty preserved fish, swap in olive tapenade or even miso paste in the same amount.

Crema di Zucca Pizzette
Pumpkin Cream Mini Pizzas

VEGETARIAN

Americans seem to think they have the market cornered on all things pumpkin when autumn rolls around, but Italians are gaga for the gourd as well—the difference is that they tend to enjoy it more in savory applications, treating it like the vegetable that it is. Zucca is classically roasted and served with brown butter and sage, or stuffed into perfect little ravioli. In the fall and winter, finding pumpkin pizza in Italy is fairly common—and it is without question one of my favorite foods on the planet.

At Berberè, a pizzeria group that specializes in a long-fermented sourdough crust and has locations in Milan, Rome, and Florence (among other cities), they decorate their zucca pizza—an autumn special—with roasted mushrooms and a hefty drizzle of housemade, rosemary-infused olive oil. I also order their honey-'nduja special sauce on the side, and the combination of flavors is sweet and spicy, herbaceous and earthy, and has been my birthday meal on more than one occasion. To replicate that here, top with roasted mushrooms, dot with 'nduja, and drizzle with honey (or, if you can't source 'nduja, Mike's Hot Honey makes a very happy substitution).

This simple miniature version of my beloved pumpkin pizza makes a perfect party snack, but there are dozens of ways to punch this up! You can top with crispy pancetta or sausage, sprinkle with grated Parmigiano Reggiano or Pecorino Romano, add roasted mushrooms or a drizzle of balsamic, or a drizzle of rosemary-infused olive oil. And of course, the pizzette format works for any other toppings you can dream up.

(CONTINUES)

Makes 6 servings

PIZZETTE

8 ounces (225 g) pizza dough (purchased from the store or your favorite pizzeria)

CREMA DI ZUCCA

1½ teaspoons (7 mL) extra-virgin olive oil

2 large cloves garlic, chopped

¼ medium shallot, chopped

8 ounces (225 g) pumpkin puree

½ cup (125 mL) heavy cream or whole milk (see Notes)

Kosher salt, q.b.

Red pepper flakes, q.b.

1 teaspoon (3 g) chopped sage leaves (fresh is preferable, but you can use dried)

ASSEMBLY

1 cup (115 to 225 g, depending on the cheese) crumbled or shredded cheese (mozzarella, scamorza, ricotta, Gorgonzola all work well; smoked cheeses are especially complementary to the sweetness of the pumpkin)

Extra-virgin olive oil, q.b.

Flake sea salt, q.b.

8 to 10 fresh sage leaves, torn in half

PREPARE THE DOUGH

Preheat the oven to 475°F / 245°C and lightly grease a sheet pan with nonstick cooking spray or oil.

On a lightly floured surface, roll the dough to about ¼ inch thick. Use a cookie or biscuit cutter to cut rounds from the dough. Re-roll scraps and repeat until all dough has been used. If using a 2- or 2½-inch cutter, you should get 15 to 18 pizzette crusts.

MAKE THE CREMA DI ZUCCA

Heat the oil in a medium frying pan over medium heat. Add the garlic and shallot and sauté until browned and softened. Transfer to a food processor and add the pumpkin puree, cream, salt, and pepper flakes. Blend until creamy, or chop by hand into a more rustic paste. Fold in the chopped sage.

ASSEMBLE AND BAKE THE PIZZETTE

Arrange the dough rounds on the sheet pan. Spread about 1 tablespoon crema di zucca on each round, then top with cheese. Drizzle with olive oil and add flakes of sea salt. Bake for about 10 minutes, until golden brown at the edges. Remove from the oven, garnish with sage leaves, and serve.

notes The crema di zucca can be warmed and used as a pasta sauce, or as a condiment for vegetables. Alternatively, store in an airtight container in the fridge for 3 to 4 days, or freeze for up to 3 months.

For a slightly different but very delicious flavor profile, substitute coconut milk for the cream.

Beer

THE OTHER ITALIAN BEVERAGE

If you're searching for early evidence of beer drinking in Italy, you can look as far south as Sicily, where in the seventh-century Phoenician traders were swapping goods while drinking suds, or as far north as Piemonte, where people may have had a handle on brewing first, as traces of a hopped beverage have emerged from around 560 B.C.E. More centrally, Romans named it *cervisia* in honor of Ceres (the goddess of crops). And still, despite this deep history, and for a country with such a rich grain culture, beer doesn't always square with what many non-Italians have in mind, i.e., a country in which wine flows through the streets like Willy Wonka's chocolate river flows through his factory.

But beer is extremely popular in Italy. In 2021 alone, Italians drank more than 20 million hectoliters, and consider it to be *the* partner for pizza. But with its degrees of carbonation and breadth of styles, weights, and ingredients, beer is ideal for any food pairing, and during aperitivo hour it's as common to see pilsner on the table as Prosecco.

In Italy, beers have historically been brewed and flavored with everything from local fruits and grains, to frutti secchi like hazelnuts and sweeteners like local honey, right up until industrialization took over. Then, for decades at the end of the twentieth century, the type of beers common in Italy were limited—mostly mass-produced lagers like Peroni or Nastro Azzurro. In the last ten years, however, the number of craft breweries has increased by more than 300 percent, and the country has developed a reputation around the world as a producer of quality craft beer.

Despite the COVID-19 pandemic compromising the industry's traction, particularly for small brewers who don't have supermarket presence and rely on on-premises sales, small brewers have shown no signs of slowing their innovation. They are bringing modern ideas to the industry while building upon the grain traditions of the country and their territories. Producers are giving new identities to Italian birre, tying their products to particular regions, as wineries do. For example, at their *birrificio agricola* (farm brewery), Ti-Mi-Li in Sicily brews with an ancient wheat from the island, along with the area's prized oranges. You can even find breweries and pizzerie collaborating—sharing grains and developing styles and flavors that will meet and partner inherently on the table.

Next time you're planning fizzy pairings, consider going beyond Prosecco. In beer—both Italian-made and others—you can discover a whole new dimension of stuzzichini-friendly sips.

5

PASTE & TORTE
Pastas and Cakes

What more could one want from life than
pasta and cakes? These recipes transform primi
like gnudi and risotto into snackable bites, make
use of ramekins and muffin tins for convenient
monoporzione (single-portion servings),
and put eggs to work in brilliant ways rarely
seen outside the brunch table.

Gnudi di Spinaci Croccanti Fritti in Padella
Crispy Pan-Fried Spinach Gnudi

VEGETARIAN

Gnudi is a classic Tuscan pasta dish, usually described as dumplings. They're cousins of gnocchi, except the latter are often made with riced potato and gnudi are ricotta-based. Traditionally, they're treated similarly to pasta, and served as a *primo* (first course) in the context of a full meal. That said, the heavenly little tufts of cheese and spinach make perfect stuzzichini when the bite-sized balls are pan-fried until crisp. Instead of tossing the pasta with butter and sage, serve on the side as a dipping sauce.

Makes about 30 gnudi

1½ cups (350 g) whole-milk ricotta

2 cups (55 g) spinach

2 large egg yolks

¼ cup (25 g) grated Parmigiano Reggiano

Nutmeg, q.b.

Kosher salt, q.b.

½ cup (50 to 60 g) 00 flour

Extra-virgin olive oil, q.b.

Unsalted butter

Chopped fresh sage leaves

Drain the ricotta and set aside.

Blanch the spinach: In a large pot of boiling salted water, cook the spinach for 2 to 3 minutes, then drain and immediately place in ice water for about 1 minute to stop the cooking process. Remove the spinach with a spider (you can then reserve the water to boil the gnudi later). Drain well and chop finely. You can use kitchen shears instead of a knife, but avoid using a food processor, which will pulverize the spinach.

In a medium mixing bowl, combine the spinach with the ricotta. Add the yolks, grated cheese, nutmeg, and salt. Mix with a rubber spatula or by hand, then gradually incorporate the flour to bind the dough. If you're working in high humidity, it might be necessary to add a little extra flour.

Turn out the dough onto a lightly floured surface and roll into balls about the size of Ping-Pong balls. Add the gnudi to the boiling water and cook for 2 to 3 minutes; drain.

Heat about ⅛ inch of oil in a medium nonstick pan over medium heat. Add the gnudi and fry, turning on all sides, until golden, 2 to 3 minutes total.

Melt the butter with the sage and use as a dipping sauce for the gnudi, with toothpicks.

Carbonara Frittatine
Carbonara-Style Mini Soufflés

GF

Given that carbonara is pasta made with egg yolk, it seems only natural to utilize the same flavor profile in an egg-based snack. Frittatine are miniature versions of frittatas, made here in a muffin tin to create a single-serving item, ideal for any spread.

Note: Beating the eggs with an electric mixer or immersion blender can yield lovely, fluffy results; however, the frittatine will puff considerably if you do so. If you go this route, don't fill the muffin cavities more than about halfway to avoid an overflow.

Makes 12 frittatine

8 large eggs

2 tablespoons (30 mL) whole milk

⅔ cup (150 g) chopped pancetta

⅔ cup (about 60 g) grated Pecorino Romano

Fresh-cracked black pepper, q.b.

Preheat the oven to 375°F / 190°C and grease a 12-cup standard muffin tin with butter or nonstick spray.

In a large bowl, beat the eggs with the milk. Stir in the pancetta and cheese and mix well. Add black pepper to taste. Fill each muffin cavity about two-thirds full. Bake for 10 to 12 minutes, until set. Serve hot or at room temperature.

Torte di Risotto
Risotto Cakes

VEGETARIAN

In Italy, it's difficult to call *un giorno* a true day if there isn't some kind of cooking, so even if you have leftovers, reheating and repurposing them is often encouraged (see also frittatine, page 157). With these little cakes, leftover risotto is reimagined: reshaped into bite-sized discs and then recooked—this time battered and fried.

It's possible to stuff these with meats or cheeses like their Roman and Sicilian cousins (suppli and arancini, respectively), or simply serve as is with a vinaigrette of your choosing. The flavor profile will be determined by the type of risotto you start with. Is it saffron-inflected Milanese? An autumnal pear and cinnamon risotto? A springy asparagus-forward option? The possibilities with a canvas like rice are boundless—you'll never tire of this one.

Makes about 9 torte

1 cup (about 250 g) prepared risotto

1 large egg

2 tablespoons (30 mL) whole milk

3 to 4 tablespoons (25 to 30 g) fresh or dried breadcrumbs

Kosher salt, q.b.

Peanut oil, for frying

Form the risotto into patties. I like them small—about the diameter of the mouth of a water glass.

Create a breading station: Beat the egg with the milk in one dish and combine the breadcrumbs with salt in a second dish. Dredge the risotto patties first in the egg to coat, then in the breadcrumbs.

In a medium nonstick frying pan, heat about 2 tablespoons oil over medium heat. In batches if necessary, fry the patties for 2 to 3 minutes on each side, until crisp and golden brown. Transfer to paper towels to drain. A spider is best for fishing them out of the oil, but a slotted spoon works well, too.

Serve with a dipping sauce like classic marinara, a pesto (page 177), or a browned butter with herbs, or even top with Pomodori Marinati (page 87) for a vinegary pop.

Sformati di Erbe & Zucchini
Herb and Zucchini Flan

GF

Sformato is a sort of savory flan that is a bit more delicate than a frittata. It may not seem like the most natural addition to the stuzzichini spread given that it demands a plate and a fork, but I'm a big fan of blending American-style brunch with Italian aperitivo, and this makes an ideal Sunday morning kind of snack, as well as a pre-dinner bite.

This is also delicious with a dollop of Crema di Parmigiano (page 30), or simply with a garnish of fresh herbs and crushed pistachios.

Makes about 6 small sformati

Extra-virgin olive oil, q.b.

1 small shallot, minced

2 large cloves garlic, minced

3 to 4 medium zucchini (about 1 pound or 450 g), sliced into thin coins

3 large eggs, separated

⅔ cup (150 mL) heavy cream

⅓ cup (about 30 g) grated cheese (like Grana Padano, Pecorino Romano, or Parmigiano Reggiano)

Kosher salt, q.b.

Fresh-cracked black pepper, q.b.

Chopped fresh mint or basil leaves, q.b.

Toasted pine nuts, for garnish (optional)

Preheat the oven to 350°F / 175°C.

Heat oil in a large nonstick frying pan over medium-high. Add the shallot and garlic and cook until translucent and fragrant. Add the zucchini and sauté until golden brown and tender, about 10 minutes. Remove from heat and cool.

In a food processor, combine the zucchini mixture with the egg yolks, cream, cheese, salt, pepper, and herbs and blend until creamy. In a separate large bowl, whip the egg whites until fluffy (by hand or with an electric mixer), then gently fold in the zucchini mixture. Pour the batter into six 3½-inch ramekins, filling each about three-fourths full. (Depending on how fluffy your batter is, you may be able to fill more than six ramekins.)

Prepare a *bagnomaria* (bain-marie, or water bath): Place the ramekins in a deep baking dish and fill the dish with water, until the ramekins are about halfway submerged. Bake for 45 to 55 minutes, until set. Let cool; attempting to remove the flans from the ramekins while too hot will likely cause them to fall apart.

When cooled to about room temperature, run a knife along the inside of each ramekin. One at a time, place a dish over the top and flip. You may have to gently tap the bottom of the ramekin to entirely extract the flan. Garnish with chopped mint or basil or toasted pine nuts, and serve.

note You can also dust the ramekins with flour or breadcrumbs before pouring in the mixture, which will help with removing the flan; just be aware this will add a crisp layer to the top and sides, which is also lovely!

Mini Muffins alle Verdure: Pomodoro & Pecorino
Savory Mini Muffins with Tomato and Pecorino

VEGETARIAN

Despite their distinct American-ness, muffins make appearances all over Italy, in both sweet and savory forms.

These muffins are similar to breakfast muffins, but a touch less sweet. The tomato and pecorino can be swapped out for just about anything you have on hand: zucchini and basil, or pine nuts and raisins, to name just a couple of options. They are also super satisfying with the addition of cured meat like pancetta, or herbs such as basil.

Makes 24 mini muffins

2 cups (240 g) all-purpose flour

¼ cup (50 g) packed brown sugar

1 tablespoon (14 g) baking powder

1 teaspoon (3 g) kosher salt

3 large eggs

2½ cups (600 mL) whole milk

1 tablespoon (15 mL) extra-virgin olive oil

¼ cup (15 g) sun-dried tomatoes, drained and chopped

⅔ cup (about 60 g) grated Pecorino Romano

Preheat the oven to 425°F / 220°C and grease a 24-cup mini muffin tin with butter or nonstick spray.

In a large bowl, combine the flour, brown sugar, baking powder, and salt. In a medium bowl, beat the eggs with the milk, then add the oil. Add to the dry ingredients and mix well. Fold in the tomatoes and cheese, reserving a small amount of cheese to sprinkle on top of the muffins.

Spoon the batter into the muffin tin, filling each cavity about two-thirds full, and sprinkle with the reserved cheese. Bake for 16 to 18 minutes, until a toothpick inserted into the center comes out clean and dry. Remove and serve warm or at room temperature.

Torta di Patate di Trentino
Trentino Potato Pancake

Mountain food in Italy has that stick-to-your-ribs quality that'll keep you upright even when trudging through the Alps or simply sitting outside with some friends and a spritz.

It might be simple, but when served with smoky speck and a dose of Prosecco from the not-so-far-away region of Veneto, these pancake wedges are a warm hug on a snowy day.

Makes about 8 servings

1⅔ pounds (750 g) potatoes (russet or similar)

Extra-virgin olive oil, q.b.

½ medium onion, chopped

2 tablespoons (15 g) all-purpose flour

Kosher salt, q.b.

⅓ cup (75 mL) whole milk

Thinly sliced speck, q.b.

Preheat the oven to 375°F / 190°C and grease a 12-inch pizza pan with nonstick spray or oil.

Grate the potatoes with a box grater, then transfer to a colander to drain.

Heat some oil in a small nonstick pan over medium heat. Add the onion and cook until golden brown and soft.

In a bowl, combine the onion and potatoes. In a separate bowl, combine the flour, salt, and milk and mix well. Combine the flour mixture with the potato mixture, incorporating until you have a homogenous blend.

Spread the mixture evenly on the prepared pan and bake for 30 minutes. Brush the top with oil, then bake another 15 to 30 minutes, until golden brown and crisp on top.

Let cool slightly. Cut into wedges and serve with speck. This is delicious served hot, but works well at room temperature, too.

note The pancake can also be made in two smaller batches and fried on the stovetop in a large, heavy-bottomed nonstick pan greased with oil. If you use this method, carefully flip the pancakes halfway through.

Torta di Ceci al Sale Marino & Olio d'Oliva
Sea Salt and Olive Oil Chickpea Pancake

VEGAN, GF

There are quite a few origin stories for this dish, each one more action-packed than the last. One stars hungry Roman soldiers frying chickpea flour on hot shields after a battle in an effort to restore their energy. Another from farther north takes a seafaring turn, purporting that during a naval battle in the thirteenth century's Genovese-Pisan War, a battered ship spilled sacks of ceci into salt water, where they were pulverized. Starving and stranded, sailors spread the mash of chickpeas on stones and, after allowing it to dry in the sun, realized they were onto something.

Today, hungry Italians seek out this crisp chickpea pancake in many regions, and refer to it by various names including *farinata, cecina,* and *socca.* Tuscans even transform this thin and custardy cornbread-esque cake into something sustaining by pan-frying slices and stuffing them into a focaccia sandwich—especially popular as street food in coastal Livorno.

Regardless of the conflicting, conflict-inspired origins, designations, and preparations, I'm certain no one will be able to fight off the craving for these crisp bites after the first taste. Serve hot as is or with a blizzard of black pepper, along with a cocktail, Prosecco, or crisp beer.

Makes 6 to 8 servings

1⅔ cups (140 g) chickpea flour

2 cups (500 mL) water

2 tablespoons (30 mL) extra-virgin olive oil

2 teaspoons (6 g) kosher salt

Chopped fresh rosemary, q.b.

Flake sea salt, q.b.

Place the chickpea flour in a large bowl and form a well. Gradually add the water, mixing well with a rubber spatula or by hand. Cover and rest at room temperature for 4 to 5 hours, or overnight, stirring occasionally. (You can skim off any foam you see forming during the resting process.)

Preheat the oven to 450°F / 230°C and grease a 12-inch pizza pan with oil.

Skim the foam from the batter a last time and discard. Whisk in the olive oil and kosher salt, spread the batter on the pan, and sprinkle with rosemary. Bake for 12 to 15 minutes, until the edges are golden brown and the top is crisp. Sprinkle with sea salt and serve hot or at room temperature.

Aperitivo in Full Color

NEON IN THE ITALIAN STYLE

Aperitivo hour in Italy is a multi-sensory experience, and despite the season or scene, when the sun sets, the lights come on—the most iconic of which may be Italy's famous neon signs. I've always been enchanted by these installations and curious about their origins, and it was in Rome at Kromos Design, in the city center, that I had a chance to learn more from Enrico Tintinago. Enrico and his brother are the fourth generation to run the family neon business, which they do along with Enrico's partner, Marianna Scaccia, as coordinator.

"After the Second World War, my great-grandfather came on the train, every time [carrying] all the elements [for each sign]," Enrico tells me. His ancestor made the journey to Rome from his home in northern Italy, where he blew and bent the tubing that would supply neon signs to his southern customers. He made double the materials for every job, as carting the delicate tubing was precarious; with duplicates, he'd be prepared if something broke in transit.

During that time, few businesses announced themselves by name. "When neon lights had [begun their use] for commercial purposes, the first thing you had to say to people was what you do: pasticceria, ristorante, bar," Enrico says. Because the signs weren't announcing a name but rather a type of establishment, his ancestor realized he could sell undamaged backups to similar businesses. From there his own enterprise grew, and he moved to Rome permanently.

Today, thanks to the staying power of neon itself, which can last for decades, some of those signs are still flickering, and are useful not only to indicate whether you'll find a selection of booze or gelato, medication or cigarettes, but also the age of a place. If the sign states the nature of the business—a gelateria, pharmacy, restaurant, or hotel—Enrico says the establishment is "probably at least thirty or forty years old."

The color of a sign can also be a distinguishing factor. "In the 1950s, neon lights came in two colors: red (neon) and blue (argon)," Enrico says, and points out that if a sign is one of those two classic hues, it's likely an older establishment. Today's signs come in all shapes and colors, as phosphorus powders can now be poured into the tubes to create vivid Aperol-esque oranges and basil-leaf greens.

And while Enrico has his own family history related to these signs, neon itself has a long relationship with aperitivo. One of the first-ever commerical neon signs, dating back to 1913, was for Cinzano, an Italian vermouth. Today, the Tintinagos and artisans like the ones at Kromos encourage their customers to consider true neon over cheaper alternatives like LED—not only for its durability, but for its significance to the culture and economy, and for the idea that purchasing from local artigiani helps maintain and connect a community. "There are people working behind the product who give real value," Enrico says.

This community-based approach is why Kromos invested in their showroom rather than moving to web-based sales. They were inspired by the original business model, and brick and mortar allows them to know their customers personally. "Think about my grandfather, with a small car driving in Rome, going to show [his product], and the link made with the customer," Enrico says, noting that the relationship between artisan and patron could endure for decades.

Today, it's nice to know that in building upon a legacy it's also possible to make something new—something you can share, face to face. No matter what you create or how you illuminate your aperitivo table, tradition, innovation, and community are elements that inspire, connect, and endure.

6

FRITTI
Fried Bites

From the northernmost regions to the very sole of the boot, Italy adores its fried foods. For reasons of economy, ease, and caloric oomph, the tradition of fritti has a long history, and for reasons of sheer crave-ability, it has a bright future, too. The following dishes are hot and crunchy and more downright delicious than any fast-food french fry, and they make your aperitivo hour into one very happy (pre-)meal.

Most of the recipes in this chapter call for peanut oil, which has a high smoke point and allows for a fast, crispy fry, but you can also use canola, grapeseed, or sunflower oil.

Salvia Fritta nella Birra
Beer-Battered Sage Leaves

VEGAN

When it comes to ingenuity and stretching ingredients into something unbelievably delicious, this dish is a prime example. Sage is common in central and northern Italy, especially around the colder months when the herb makes its way into the likes of pumpkin ravioli and brown butter sauces. But here the simplicity of the beer-battered herb is a reminder that, at one time, the desire to stretch a humble leaf into something calorically sustaining could result in an unforgettable creation as well. The battered and fried leaves are puffy and golden brown, crunchy and salty and herbaceous, and guests may be surprised to find them on the table as a snack rather than a garnish, but I guarantee that they will make a lasting impression.

Makes 6 to 8 servings

2 cups (500 mL) peanut oil, for frying

½ cup (about 20) fresh sage leaves

1½ cups (180 g) all-purpose flour

1⅔ cups (400 mL) cold beer (crisp lager, preferably) or sparkling water

Kosher salt, q.b.

Fresh-cracked black pepper, q.b.

Flake sea salt, for serving, q.b.

Heat the peanut oil in a heavy-bottomed frying pan to about 350°F / 175°C. Wash the sage leaves gently and pat dry with a paper towel.

In a mixing bowl, combine the flour and beer (or water) with kosher salt and pepper and mix until smooth. Dip each leaf in the batter, removing excess.

Working in batches, place the leaves in the hot oil, well-spaced, and fry until golden and crisp on each side, 1 to 2 minutes. They will puff slightly. Remove from the oil and lay the sage on a clean, dry paper towel. A spider works best for this, but you can also use a slotted spoon.

Sprinkle generously with sea salt and serve warm.

Sardine Fritte
Fried Sardines

In various parts of the peninsula you'll find an array of fried fish served in cones with long skewers with which to spear them for snacking. You can serve these sardines with a red pesto or vinaigrette as a dipping sauce, but a squeeze of lemon usually gets the job done just as well. This recipe also works with squid, anchovies, and shrimp (see Note). If you have time and access, make it seafood fritti misti and serve with a cold pilsner on a summer day.

Makes 6 to 8 servings

5 to 7 fresh sardines (¾ to 1 pound or 350 to 450 g), cleaned

1 cup (120 g) all-purpose flour

⅔ cup (100 g) cornmeal

Kosher salt, q.b.

Fresh-cracked black pepper, q.b.

Peanut oil, for frying

Lemon, for squeezing

Chopped fresh parsley, for garnish

Dry the sardines well with paper towels. In a medium mixing bowl, sift the flour, cornmeal, and salt and pepper together. Dredge each fish through the mixture, coating evenly on both sides.

In a medium heavy-bottomed pan, heat about 2 inches peanut oil over medium-high heat until it sizzles when tested with a few breadcrumbs (about 375°F / 190°C). In batches, fry the sardines for about 2 minutes on each side, until crisp and golden brown. Transfer to clean paper towels to drain. A spider works best for removing the fish, but a slotted spoon works as well.

Salt, squeeze lemon over the top, and garnish with parsley. Serve hot.

note If you'd prefer to do a fritto misto, or an alternate seafood, the following are some different fry times:

CALAMARI (BOTH RINGS AND TENTACLES): about 3 minutes

FRESH ANCHOVIES: about 1 minute each side

JUMBO SHRIMP: 3 to 4 minutes

Mozzarella in Carrozza al Pesto
Mozzarella in a Carriage with Pesto

 VEGETARIAN

Fried mozzarella is a standard in American red sauce joints and fast casual restaurants these days, but this preparation, which shares more DNA with a croque monsieur than mozzarella sticks, is the kind of Italian cooking that presents as "rustic," but still requires real finesse and care. The process of breading and resting the sandwiches, then breading them again, is a bit labor intensive, but the result is worth it: The cheese, which stays sealed inside rather than running out the edges, is like a prize to be discovered beneath the extra crunchy crust.

This recipe is for a *semplice* (simple) version, but you can also layer additions into the sandwiches. Sun-dried tomatoes, roasted red peppers, protein (like anchovies, 'nduja, or prosciutto), and herbs (like basil or thyme) are all delicious. If you're adding fillings, make sure to do so before quartering the sandwiches, doing your best to place each ingredient within the confines of where you'll make the cuts.

Serve the sandwiches with the pesto or your favorite marinara sauce as a dip. They are also delicious with a drizzle of Balsamic Glaze (page 83) or Cherry Mostarda (page 184).

Makes 16 small sandwiches

MOZZARELLA IN CARROZZA

12 ounces (340 g) fresh mozzarella (day-old is preferable, as it will be slightly drier)

8 slices soft white bread

Kosher salt, q.b.

1 cup (120 g) all-purpose flour

3 large eggs

2½ cups (300 g) fresh or dried breadcrumbs

Peanut oil (if frying)

PESTO GENOVESE

2 tablespoons (20 g) pine nuts

2 cups (40 g) fresh basil leaves, chopped

¼ cup (25 g) grated Pecorino Romano

¼ cup (25 g) grated Parmigiano Reggiano

2 large cloves garlic, peeled

¼ cup (60 mL) extra-virgin olive oil

¼ cup (60 mL) lemon juice

MAKE THE MOZZARELLA IN CARROZZA

Cut the mozzarella into ¼-inch-thick slices and use a paper towel to dry each slice well. The less moisture, the better, so the cheese and bread will adhere to one another and make the breading process neater and more effective.

Arrange four slices of bread on a cutting board and lay cheese slices on each piece of bread (usually three or four slices will cover the surface, depending on the size of your mozzarella ball). Salt the cheese layer and cover with the remaining four slices of bread to create sandwiches. Use a bread knife to trim the crusts (reserve to make breadcrumbs) and cut each sandwich into quarters or triangles.

Prepare a breading station: Place the flour in one dish, beat the eggs in a second dish, and place the breadcrumbs in a third. Compress each sandwich well with your hands, then dredge through the flour, then the eggs (draining any excess well), and then the breadcrumbs. Rest the sandwiches in the refrigerator for about 30 minutes to make sure the batter sets and adheres well.

Remove the sandwiches from the refrigerator and dredge through the egg and then the breadcrumbs again for a double batter and extra crispy crust. Rest again in the refrigerator for 30 minutes. This allows the batter to set up well and will prevent it from flaking off during the cooking process.

There are a number of options for cooking the sandwiches until crisp and golden brown:

OPTION 1: Deep-fry in a large saucepan, with peanut oil heated to 350°F / 175°C, for about 2 minutes. Drain on paper towels.

OPTION 2: Pan-fry in a shallow layer of peanut oil, carefully flipping, for about 1 minute on each side.

OPTION 3: Bake on a greased sheet pan at 400°F / 205°C, for 6 to 8 minutes.

OPTION 4: Spray an air fryer basket with nonstick spray. Air fry the sandwiches at 390°F / 200°C for 5 minutes, then flip and fry for another 3 minutes.

MAKE THE PESTO GENOVESE

Toast the pine nuts in a small frying pan over medium heat. Using a mortar and pestle, or in a food processor, combine the pine nuts with the basil, cheese, and garlic until well-integrated. Gradually drizzle in the olive oil and lemon juice until a paste is formed.

note The pesto is a fairly thick, paste-like version of the sauce, which I like as a starting point. If you prefer a thinner option, drizzle in additional oil until the desired consistency is achieved.

Pesto Personalities

Like so many regional specialties, pesto has been flattened into a single flavor profile—one played by basil and pine nuts. And while this Genovese interpretation is indeed delicious, it is far from the only one.

Almost any combination of herb, nut, fat, and cheese will get the job done. You can also manipulate more than the flavor profile: Are you looking for something thinner and more like a vinaigrette? Use more oil. Prefer more of a paste or spread? Amp up the solids. No matter how you slice it (or smash or puree it), you won't be disappointed.

ALTERNATIVE PESTO SUGGESTIONS

Arugula and almonds

Cilantro and peanut with cotija cheese

Parsley and walnuts

Sorrel and pumpkin seeds

Mint and pistachios

Dill and feta

Cubetti di Polenta
Crispy Polenta Cubes

VEGAN, GF

Like risotto, polenta makes for fantastic leftovers. And while reheating polenta in its pure form is delicious on its own, these breaded and fried little cubes give fresh life to yesterday's lunch.

Serve hot or cold with a balsamic drizzle, Caramelized Onion Jam (page 57) and speck, or Crema di Gorgonzola Dolce (page 63). Serve on a stick with fondue or Crema di Parmigiano (page 30), or simply enjoy fresh from the oil with a bit of salt or even a dusting of powdered sugar. These are an inarguable delight in any scenario.

Makes 6 to 8 servings

1 cup (150 g) cornmeal (polenta)

Peanut oil, for shallow frying

Kosher salt, q.b.

Ground chili powder, q.b. (optional)

Prepare the polenta according to package instructions, then spread onto a parchment-lined sheet pan to about 1 inch thick using a rubber spatula. Allow to cool completely.

When fully cooled, cut the polenta into small cubes, about 1 inch square. Fill a large nonstick pan with enough peanut oil to cover the bottom and heat over medium-high heat. Fry the cubes, turning them throughout the process, until golden brown and crisp on all sides, 7 to 10 minutes in total. Drain on paper towels, then sprinkle with salt and chili powder (if using) and serve hot.

You can also make a baked version of these little bites: Arrange the cubes on a parchment-lined sheet pan, leaving space in between each. Bake in a 425°F / 220°C oven for about 15 minutes, then flip and bake for another 15 minutes, until golden brown and crispy.

Olive Ascolane
Ascolana-Style Fried Olives

Give the mini Marche region a very big high five for handing the world these unbelievably satisfying olives. So proud are its people of this creation that they hold an annual festival for three days in August to celebrate their very existence—complete with expert speakers, workshops, and demonstrations about the particulars of the olive and its history. There's even a sort of theme song (see the box below).

As always, Italians know how to stretch an ingredient and repurpose. Olive Ascolane do double duty: They're a great way to utilize any meat lying around, and also make a meal out of a simple fruit.

(CONTINUES)

A Stuzzichini Soundtrack

These days, we have the luxury of purchasing pitted olives, but for most of this dish's history, the tedious job had to be done by hand. Fortunately, the women who historically prepared this dish (and they were most likely *always* women) were creative with how to pass the time. Allegedly, they sang the following tune to keep their spirits high while they rolled up their sleeves.

Though the lyrics are in a local dialect and difficult to translate clearly, the essence of the song is a list of ingredients and steps (along with some advice, like to be careful when handling the lemon rind). Today, buying pitted olives will certainly speed the process, but I'm sure no one will fault you for singing anyway.

Tira jó la cazzarola,

mitte l'olie e la cepolla,

coratina e senneritte.

Falli sfrie, eppuó ce mitte

carne fresca, parte uguale:

pulle, manze e lu maiale,

magra, scedda e fatt'a piezze.

Se vuó dagghie più sapore,

puó calà lu fegatielle

de'nu pulle raspatore.

'Nu cucó de bianche sicche,

che svapora e 'nsaperisce.

Sale e pepe, e all'uddem'ora,

'nu cicì de pemmadora.

Passa la ciccia su la
'mmacchenetta

dó vodde, che ccusci te vè
più fina,

la mitte dentre 'na
curtescianetta

ce scule lu seghitte suó passate,

'n' uove sbattute e la noce
m'scata.

Ce ratte 'nu ccunille de limone,

sule la scorza gialla, fa
'ttenzione!

'nu bielle ccó de cace
ratteggiate:

'na parte de pecuri de lu Ciafò,

e dó de parmeggià, senza la
cocchia.

e se ttié 'nu tartefitte,

te lu ratte e ce lu mitte!

Tiellu da parte, e lu repiene
è fatte!!

Makes 6 to 8 servings

FILLING

Extra-virgin olive oil, q.b.

½ medium onion, chopped

1 medium carrot, chopped

1 medium stalk celery, chopped

¼ pound (115 g) ground beef

¼ pound (115 g) ground pork

¼ pound (115 g) ground chicken

1 cup (250 mL) white wine

Kosher salt, q.b.

¾ cup (75 g) grated cheese (Parmigiano Reggiano, Pecorino Romano, Grana Padano)

¼ cup (30 g) breadcrumbs

Grated zest of 1 lemon

Pinch ground nutmeg

Pinch cloves

1 large egg, beaten

OLIVES

6 to 7 cups (850 g to 1 kg) olives, pitted

1½ cups (180 g) all-purpose flour

2 large eggs, beaten

1½ cups (180 g) fresh or dried bread crumbs

Peanut oil, for frying

MAKE THE FILLING

Heat oil in a medium frying pan over medium heat. Add the sofrito (onion, carrot, and celery) and cook until softened and fragrant. Add all the meat and cook until browned. Add the white wine and continue to cook over low heat until the meat is cooked through and the liquid is mostly evaporated, but not totally dry, about 10 minutes. Remove from the heat and allow to cool. Run through a food processor until you have a homogenous mixture. Salt to taste (but be cautious not to overdo it, as the briny olives pack a salty punch!).

Transfer the mixture to a bowl and add the cheese, breadcrumbs, lemon zest, nutmeg, and cloves. Stir in the egg. Work the mixture together into a ball, then cover and rest for 25 minutes in the refrigerator.

STUFF, BREAD, AND FRY THE OLIVES

Stuff each olive with the meat mixture; you'll need to push the filling into the opening in each olive by hand.

Set up your breading station: one dish with the flour, a second dish with the beaten eggs, and a third with the breadcrumbs. Dredge the olives through the breading station (flour, then egg, then breadcrumbs), then refrigerate for about 20 minutes to allow batter to set up.

Heat about 2 inches of oil in a medium frying pan over medium-high heat until it sizzles when tested with a bit of breadcrumbs (about 375°F / 190°C). Add the breaded olives and fry in batches, rotating throughout the process, until golden brown all over, 4 to 5 minutes.

Remove the olives from the oil with a spider or slotted spoon and drain on paper towels. Serve hot or at room temperature.

note Ascolana Tenera olives are traditional, but any large, firm variety will work well.

Coccole con Mostarda
"Cuddles" with Mostarda

VEGAN

One of my favorite Italian words of all time, *coccole,* means "cuddles." What else could better describe little balls of warm and crispy fried dough? They pair beautifully with an array of meats and cheeses, as well as mostarda—a sweet and spicy condiment that comes in a variety of flavors (see the recipe for Cherry Mostarda on page 184). Or drizzle with a marinara and dust with grated cheese for little fried pizza hugs. But I've also enjoyed coccole served in sweeter preparations, like stuffed with dates and soft cheeses and drizzled with honey and/or chocolate.

Makes 6 to 8 servings

1 tablespoon (10 g) active dry yeast

1 cup (250 mL) warm water

1 teaspoon (5 g) granulated sugar

3⅓ cups (400 g) all-purpose flour

Peanut oil, for frying

Kosher salt, q.b.

Line a sheet pan with Silpat or parchment paper.

In a small bowl, bloom the yeast in about ¼ cup of the warm water, about 10 minutes. Add the sugar and combine.

Place the flour in a large mixing bowl and create a well. Pour the yeast mixture into the well, then knead, gradually adding the remaining warm water. Knead into a dough ball, cover, and rest in a warm place for about 2 hours.

Form the dough into about 12 balls, 1 to 1½ inches in diameter, and arrange on the sheet pan, allowing space in between. Allow to rise for 30 minutes.

In a heavy-bottomed pan, heat about 2 inches of peanut oil over medium-high heat until about 375°F / 190°C. Add the balls and fry in batches, turning throughout, until all sides are golden and crispy, about 5 minutes. Drain on paper towels, salt, and serve hot.

Mostarda di Ciliegie
Cherry Mostarda

 VEGAN, GF

Mostarda is a classic condiment in Italy, particularly for aperitivo, served as an accompaniment to cheese and cured meats on *tagliere* (boards). It is typically made with some kind of fruit, sugar syrup, and spices—particularly mustard powder or essential oil, hence the name—making it beguilingly complex and layered. It can range widely in preparation, flavor, and consistency, though. Occasionally vegetables take the place of fruit. At times, it's close to a jam—spreadable and thick with crushed or pureed fruit. At others, you can find whole pieces of fruit sitting in a spiced sugar syrup. Though mostarda does feature mustard seed, either whole or in powder form, it is nothing like the neon yellow or Dijon versions we're used to in the States, and the heat level from the mustard might be barely perceptible, purely balancing, or bracing and intense.

This recipe is a great starting point for you to taste and modify as you like. You can crank up the mustard powder or even use mustard essential oil (which appears in commercial versions); or change up the fruit and decide whether you prefer larger pieces, or more of a puree.

No matter how you spin it, mostarda, with its sweet and spicy flavor profile, has great range as a condiment. It's a perfect complement to crispy and chewy coccole, as well as cheeses and meats, but it's also delicious on eggs, seared onto a pork chop, tossed into a roasted vegetable dish, or simply spread on toast.

Makes about 1½ cups mostarda

1⅓ cups (210 g) pitted cherries

2 tablespoons (25 g) granulated sugar

1½ tablespoons (20 mL) white wine

1 tablespoon (15 mL) cider vinegar (or juice of ½ lemon)

Kosher salt, q.b.

1½ tablespoons (16 g) mustard powder

Red pepper flakes, q.b. (optional)

In a medium saucepan, simmer the cherries with the sugar, wine, vinegar, and a dash of salt for 12 to 15 minutes, until softened. Remove from the heat and stir in the mustard powder and the pepper flakes if using. Allow to cool and serve.

Keep any remaining mostarda in an airtight container in the refrigerator for up to a month.

Crocchette di Granchio con Vinaigrette agli Agrumi Strega
Crab Fritters with Strega Citrus Vinaigrette

One can find a recipe for crab in Italy going back to the fifth century in the pages of the ancient Roman cookbook *Apicius.* Today, it is not uncommon to find it utilized in pasta and risotto dishes, and you can even take a watery tour to find the famous moeche crab of the Venetian Lagoon—a feature of the ecotourism industry in Italy.

Regardless of which country you find yourself in, it's hard to argue with the fact that this crustacean makes for damn fine fritti. This preparation is a close relative of the American crab cake, and the vinaigrette, containing the herbal Liquore Strega (made with more than seventy botanicals, including mint, saffron, and juniper), provides an acidic boost.

Makes 25 to 30 crocchette

STREGA CITRUS VINAIGRETTE

3 tablespoons (45 mL) Liquore Strega

Grated zest and juice of ½ blood orange (or any other citrus)

2 teaspoons (15 mL) honey

Kosher salt, q.b.

Fresh-cracked black pepper, q.b.

½ cup (125 mL) extra-virgin olive oil

CROCCHETTE DI GRANCHIO

2 medium potatoes (½ pound or 225 g), peeled and cubed

Extra-virgin olive oil, q.b.

2 large cloves garlic, minced

12 ounces (340 g) crabmeat

1 large egg, beaten

Grated zest of 1 lemon

Fresh basil and/or thyme leaves, q.b.

Red pepper flakes (1 teaspoon or 3 g, or q.b.), optional

Kosher salt, q.b.

Fresh-cracked black pepper, q.b.

1½ cups (180 g) dried or fresh breadcrumbs

Peanut oil, for frying

MAKE THE VINAIGRETTE

In a small bowl, whisk together the Liquore Strega, citrus zest and juice, and honey with salt and pepper. Gradually incorporate the oil until well emulsified.

Serve with the crocchette, or store in an airtight container in the fridge for up to 2 weeks. This dressing can be used in all the ways you apply your favorite vinaigrettes—to dress salads, marinate meats or veggies, or drizzle over bruschette.

MAKE THE CROCCHETTE

Cook the potatoes in a large pot of boiling water for about 20 minutes, until tender. Drain and puree in a food processor or coarsely mash, depending on preference and tools.

Heat oil in a large nonstick frying pan over medium heat. Add the garlic and sauté until browned. Add the crabmeat and continue to cook for 2 to 3 minutes, until heated through. Transfer to a medium bowl, stir in the potatoes using a rubber spatula, and allow to cool.

Add the egg, lemon zest, herbs, and pepper flakes (if using) to the cooled crab mixture, then salt and pepper to taste. If necessary, add a bit of breadcrumbs to bind. Form into 25 to 30 balls and flatten slightly into fritters. One by one, dredge them in breadcrumbs.

In a heavy-bottomed pan, heat about 1 inch peanut oil over medium-high heat until it sizzles when tested with a bit of breadcrumbs (about 375°F / 190°C). In batches, add the crocchette and fry until golden brown and crispy on each side, about 3 minutes. Remove from the oil with a spider or slotted spoon and drain on paper towels.

Serve hot with a simple squeeze of lemon, more fresh basil, or the vinaigrette.

note If you can't find Strega, or don't want to invest in a full bottle, you can use any number of liqueurs you may have on hand, including limoncello, Galliano, Luxardo Maraschino, Grand Marnier, or Pernod. Each will bring its own unique flavor profile, but it's fun to experiment!

Ladin's Love Language

There are parts of northern Italy where trying to have a simple conversation might confound even native speakers. In this area, borders have shifted repeatedly throughout history, and in the course of those cultural exchanges a community known as Ladin emerged. The Ladin people are known for traditions deeply rooted in a relationship with nature, and reflect a conflation of both northern and southern European influences. These philosophies and characteristics are manifest through folklore and art, conservation efforts and craftsmanship—all through an ancient language that has similarities to Romansh and Friulian dialects, but is entirely its own. Today, the language considered "Ladin," which is believed to have roots as far back as the first century, is recognized and protected by the Italian parliament, but is spoken by only about 30,000 Italians.

Despite efforts by Fascist forces to stamp it out, as well as the implementation of an Italian national language—not to mention the relentless march of time—Ladin life persists. Three present-day enclaves exist. One is in the Swiss Engadin Valley, and two are in Italy: in Friuli and in the Dolomites, with the Fassa, Gardena, and Badia valleys and Fodom/Livinallongo in Veneto the most significant among them.

And while these communities continue to tell a story of Italy's past, a rich philosophy of hospitality helps them remain connected to the modern world. "The inhabitants of Alta Badia are very close to their culture and traditions," says Nicole Dorigo, a publicist representing this area of the Italian Alps. But Nicole also explains that the locals want to showcase that culture for tourists, and they see their culinary traditions as being one way to do so. "The young generations are willing to maintain the customs and to cultivate the old traditions," she says. But she adds, "There are also young chefs or gourmet chefs who take inspiration from the Ladin cuisine to create new dishes served in gourmet or Michelin-starred restaurants."

Regardless of language, Ladin food is very much in conversation with the world around its people, past and present. "The Ladin cuisine is a very genuine cuisine," Nicole says. "The dishes are made with simple ingredients that the farmers cultivated in their garden or at the farm (for example, meat from their own animals, flour, vegetables like spinach and sauerkraut, milk products for the ricotta cheese, et cetera)." And the simplicity of the food speaks deliciously for itself. Mountain butters made by hand, rich dumplings (similar to gnudi, like the hand pies here), dishes made with smoky speck and local cheeses—they all help spin tales about a particular slice of Italian history while appealing to the modern palate and hunger for discovery.

My aperitivo experiences in parts of Ladin country—namely Friuli, Cortina d'Ampezzo, and Alta Badia—left a deep impression, and a hunger for more. And while the Ladin language might feel hopelessly foreign to many, it's a snap to translate Ladin-style dishes to the stuzzichini table, whether with specific combinations and ingredients, or simply by honoring the philosophy of connecting with the land and people around you. In particular, *tutres,* these spinach hand pies, make a perfect aperitivo addition. (The recipe was shared with me by Nicole on behalf of the Alta Badia region.)

Ladin Tutres
Ladin-Style Spinach Hand Pies

VEGETARIAN

"The Ladin cuisine is a very simple but genuine one, with the recipes passed on from mother to daughter, from generation to generation," says Nicole Dorigo of the northern Italian culture. "Nowadays, Ladin dishes are still cooked at home and tourists have the possibility to experience it [by] having lunch or dinner at very special local restaurants, [or] in typical farms where people still live and work.

"One of my favorite dishes [are the] fried pastries filled with ricotta cheese and spinach. Traditionally, people ate them with barley soup, [but today they are] also served as an aperitif, paired with a fantastic South Tyrolean white wine, like an Alto Adige Gewürztraminer."

This recipe has been slightly modified for American tools and measurements, based on an original from AltaBadia.org. Nicole says sauerkraut is a traditional accompaniment for tutres, but I've also enjoyed them simply dressed with a punchy vinaigrette, or even a side of applesauce. In any case, they invoke the crisp Alpine air and are clear evidence of a thoughtful, hospitable culture.

Makes 12 to 15 tutres

DOUGH

1½ cups (200 g) rye flour

¾ cup (100 g) all-purpose flour

1 large egg

2 tablespoons (30 g) unsalted butter, melted

Kosher salt, q.b.

About 2 tablespoons (30 mL) lukewarm water, q.b.

FILLING

Unsalted butter, q.b.

½ small onion, chopped

1 large clove garlic, minced

¾ cup (about 150 g) cooked (sautéed or steamed) spinach, minced

Kosher salt, q.b.

Fresh-cracked black pepper, q.b.

Nutmeg, q.b.

½ cup (120 g) whole-milk ricotta

FRYING

Peanut oil, q.b.

MAKE THE DOUGH

In a large bowl, mix together all the dough ingredients. You can use a stand mixer with a dough hook here, but it will come together into an elastic dough by hand as well. Cover and rest the dough on the countertop for 1 hour.

Roll the dough on a lightly floured surface until about ⅛ inch thick and cut out rounds. Traditionally, these would be about 5 inches in diameter (and ⅛ inch thick), but you can scale as you like! Just be sure to cut an even number of rounds.

MAKE THE FILLING

In a medium saucepan, melt about ½ tablespoon butter over medium heat. Add the onion and garlic and sauté until translucent. Add the spinach and season with salt, pepper, and nutmeg. Transfer to a medium mixing bowl and allow to cool to room temperature. Stir in the ricotta.

MAKE AND FRY THE TUTRES

Fill a large, heavy-bottomed pot about halfway with peanut oil and heat to 365°F / 185°C.

Place 1 heaping tablespoon of the filling in the center of half of the dough rounds. Cover each with another round and push carefully with your fingers along the edges to seal. (I like to use a fork here to aid the process.)

Add the pies to the hot oil, four or five at a time (as your pot allows without crowding), and fry for about 5 minutes, flipping as needed, until golden brown and crisp. Use a spider to remove the pies as they finish frying, and drain on paper towels. Serve warm or at room temperature.

7

DOLCI
Sweets

Aperitivo is technically a pre-meal tradition.
That said, as more people adopt the practice of
apericena—or stretching their stuzzichini and
small bites into a full meal—I find that there's
room to offer a little something sweet to bring the
experience to a close. Here are a few that fit the
bill without straying too far from the stuzzichini
format.

Bocconcini di Mascarpone Popcorn Dolci & Salati

Sweet and Salty Popcorn Mascarpone Bites

Once upon a time, I owned an ice cream shop very far from Italy, in a land known as Brooklyn. At the Hay Rosie Craft Ice Cream Company, we experimented with ways to add flavor to our products without altering an obsessively dialed-in ice cream base. One of the most effective ways to do this was to infuse the cream itself with an ingredient (nuts, flowers, herbs, et cetera) and then strain out the solids, leaving only the essence behind. Fat is an amazing carrier of flavor, which makes cream an ideal canvas for just about any inspiration, but my favorite was a popcorn-infused ice cream.

When I moved to Italy and found popcorn so prevalent during aperitivo hour, I couldn't shake the thought of a play on this idea as a sweet-and-salty stuzzichino. These bites bring that technique to the table.

The addition of luscious mascarpone thickens the popcorn-infused cream, which holds up well when served on toasted, buttery brioche rather than in an ice cream cone.

These pair really well with an herbaceous Hugo Spritz (page 232), but the effervescence of a simple sparkling wine will keep your palate fresh for each sweet and salty bite, too.

Makes 6 to 8 servings

POPCORN-INFUSED CREAM

1½ cups (350 mL) heavy cream

1 teaspoon (3 g) kosher salt

1 cup (about 10 g) freshly popped popcorn (see Notes), plus more for garnish

POPCORN MASCARPONE CREAM

¾ cup (85 g) powdered sugar

1 teaspoon (5 g) sea salt

1 cup (240 g) mascarpone, chilled

BOCCONCINI

Brioche, cut into bite-sized pieces (about 1½-inch squares or triangles), q.b.

Unsalted butter, q.b.

Fresh mint or basil leaves, q.b. (optional)

MAKE THE POPCORN-INFUSED CREAM

In a small saucepan, bring the cream to a low simmer. Stir in the salt and popped corn, which will "deflate." Remove from the heat and allow to infuse for about 2 hours.

Strain out the popcorn using a fine mesh sieve, pushing on the kernels to wring out as much cream as possible. You will lose some of the volume and will need about 1 cup (250 mL) infused cream to make the mascarpone cream. If you come up a bit shy, you can always add a splash of unflavored cream; it will dilute the flavor just slightly.

MAKE THE POPCORN MASCARPONE CREAM

It's easiest to make whipped cream using a stand or hand mixer, if available, but you can do this by hand—it'll just take a bit of elbow grease and patience. Since cold temperatures help trap the air bubbles needed for a light and airy cream, it helps to chill your mixing bowl in advance.

Place 1 cup popcorn-infused cream, the powdered sugar, and the salt in a medium mixing bowl and beat (on medium-high if using an electric mixer) until soft peaks form. Add the mascarpone and continue whipping until stiff peaks form.

(CONTINUES)

ASSEMBLE THE BOCCONCINI

In a medium frying pan, lightly toast the brioche pieces in butter; let cool completely.

To assemble, use a piping bag or teaspoon to portion the popcorn mascarpone onto the toasted brioche and garnish with a fresh piece of popcorn. Mint and basil make for a beautiful and fragrant touch as well, if you'd like a little extra flair.

notes It's important that the popcorn be freshly popped, as the aromas and flavors are most potent when warm and toasty.

The popcorn cream is also delicious as a whipped cream all on its own, or as an ingredient for a gelato base.

Ciliegie Affogate alla Sambuca
Sambuca-Poached Cherries

 VEGAN, GF

Sambuca and cherries both remind me of my grandfather, who appreciated the fruit and the drink separately but with an equal sense of joy. I think he'd have loved this recipe, in which they join forces. While brandied cherries are more common, I adore the anise-tinted taste of sambuca with the stone fruit. Together, they bring depth to a cocktail as a garnish, but are equally delicious as a topping for gelato or crostini with whipped ricotta, or straight from a toothpick.

Makes 1 pound cherries

1 pound (450 g) fresh cherries (about 2½ cups pitted without stems)

½ cup (125 mL) water

⅓ cup (65 g) granulated sugar

Juice of 1 medium lemon

1 ounce (about 30 mL) sambuca

Wash and pit cherries.

In a saucepan, combine the water, sugar, lemon juice, and sambuca and simmer until dissolved. Add the cherries and cook for about 15 minutes, until softened.

Cherries can be stored in a jar in the fridge for a few days.

Agrumi Canditi
Candied Citrus

 VEGAN, GF

If necessity is the mother of invention, perhaps waste aversion is the nonna of Italian culinary ingenuity. Living in Italy taught me how to utilize every inch of an ingredient, and these citrus peels—which normally go in the compost bin back in the U.S.—might as well be solid gold. You can find candied citrus in stores and pasticcerie, but also baked into panettone, or folded into gelato. I love the strips on their own as a snack, but their bittersweet flavor also happens to work wonders as a cocktail garnish, and even adds dimension as bright little pops of flavor when chopped up and tossed into a salad or sprinkled over pate on bruschette.

If you're so inclined, you can also bake them into breakfast goodies or use them to top cakes (or panettone) or cap cannoli, and—either as is, or dipped in chocolate—they make a lovely little dolce to set out in the event your guests linger past apericena and need a bite for dessert.

Makes 8 to 10 servings (about 1 cup candied peels)

6 to 8 citrus fruits (lemon, orange, grapefruit—whatever you have on hand; see Notes)

1 cup (250 mL) water, room temperature

1½ cups (300 g) granulated sugar

Top and tail the citrus with a sharp knife, then remove the zest (the colored part of the peel), leaving behind as much of the white pith as possible. Cut the zest into thin strips.

Bring a medium saucepan of water to a boil. Add the strips and cook for about 10 minutes. Drain, then repeat this boil-and-drain process twice more, with the goal of removing some of the bitterness. Drain the strips one final time and set aside.

Using the same saucepan, combine the 1 cup water with 1 cup (200 g) of the sugar and boil until dissolved. Return the drained zest strips to the pot and return to a boil. Simmer for 40 to 50 minutes, until the peels are softened and the syrup is reduced. Drain the zest strips (reserve the syrup; see Notes), then toss with the remaining ½ cup (100 g) sugar.

Spread on a sheet pan in a single layer, shaking off any excess sugar. Allow the strips to dry overnight on the counter. (If you happen to have a dehydrator, this is a great time to use it!) Store in an airtight container for up to one month.

notes Ideally, the citrus has been reserved from another use or recipe, like Salsa Garibaldi (page 218) or a cocktail, but make sure your leftovers still have their peel.

Save the syrup! You can use it for cocktails, to drizzle on cakes, or even cook into an agrodolce for broccoli or beets.

Sorbetto alla Vaniglia Aperol
Aperol Vanilla Sorbet

 VEGAN, GF

Though Italians drink spritzes all year round, it has become somewhat a de facto symbol of summery weather in the U.S. This frozen twist leans into that vibe, with the addition of vanilla for the nostalgic Creamsicle kick we all know and love.

See the Note for a granita variation in case you don't have an ice cream maker.

Makes 4 to 6 servings

4 to 6 medium oranges

3 cups (700 mL) orange juice (6 to 8 oranges)

⅔ cup (135 g) granulated sugar

3½ tablespoons (50 mL) Aperol

1 vanilla bean, seeds scraped

Whipped cream, for garnish

Fresh mint leaves, for garnish

Prepare the oranges and orange juice: Cut the tops off the oranges (¼ to ½ inch) and set the tops aside for another use. Use a sharp knife to carve out the pulp of the fruit, cutting around the perimeter and removing as much as possible while keeping the skin intact. Set the "cups" in the freezer for later use. Press the pulp for juice.

In a small saucepan over medium-high heat, bring about ½ cup (125 mL) juice and the sugar to a simmer, stirring until dissolved. Remove from the heat and mix in the Aperol and remaining juice. Chill thoroughly (overnight is best).

Stir the vanilla bean seeds (reserve the pod for other uses!) into the juice mixture. Freeze in an ice cream maker according to manufacturer's instructions.

Spoon the ice cream into the frozen orange cups. Serve with whipped cream and a garnish of fresh mint.

note If you don't have an ice cream maker, you can make granita from this mixture. Using a metal 9x13-inch sheet pan, pour the chilled mixture onto the pan in a thin layer, then place in the freezer. Use a fork to periodically scrape the mixture as it freezes into icy crystals over the course of about 1 hour. Chill for another 3 to 4 hours and serve in orange cups with whipped cream and a garnish of fresh mint.

Gelo di Melone
Sicilian Watermelon Pudding

VEGAN, GF

Stroll the streets of Palermo in summer and you can find this creamy, spoonable treat all over the place. Easy to make, refreshing as all hell (especially when the weather feels like you may be in the seventh circle of it), and customizable with a variety of toppings. Exercise your right to add a little maraschino liqueur, and you can see why this unusual pudding might fall into heavy summer rotation.

Makes about 4 servings

3½ to 4 cups (500 to 600g) cubed and seeded fresh watermelon, or more if needed

⅓ cup (65 g) granulated sugar

3 tablespoons (25 g) cornstarch

1 teaspoon (5 mL) vanilla extract

2 tablespoons (30 mL) maraschino liqueur (like Luxardo), optional

Whipped cream, chopped chocolate, pistachios, Candied Citrus (page 200), for garnish, optional

Use a food processor or blender to juice the watermelon, then press well through a fine mesh sieve, squeezing out as much juice out as possible. You'll need about 2 cups (500 mL) juice to work with, so if you need it, juice a little more.

In a medium saucepan, combine the juice, sugar, and cornstarch and stir until dissolved. Simmer for about 5 minutes over medium-high heat, whisking regularly, until the mixture thickens. Reduce heat and cook until the mixture coats the back of a spoon (similar to a curd). Remove from the heat, stir in the vanilla (and liqueur if using), then portion into jars.

Cover with plastic and chill in the refrigerator; the pudding will set in 3 to 4 hours. To serve, top with whipped cream, then chocolate, pistachios, and/or candied citrus.

Biscotti di Hugo
Hugo Cookies

 **VEGETARIAN, GF (IF USING RICE FLOUR)**

Lime is a relatively new addition to the Italian flavor canon. For most of history it was only available as an import, which made it expensive (not to mention antithetical to most Italian lifestyles and beliefs).

Because of the changing climate, the fruit—which typically thrives in tropical climates—has begun to find hospitable environments in parts of southern Italy, including Sicily and Calabria, and has made its way into the culinary repertoire. Naturally, that means cocktails, too.

These cookies are inspired by the Hugo Spritz (page 232). When I first tasted the drink at a bar in Florence's Oltrarno (the side of the Arno River opposite the city center) on a summer day, I felt the flavor profile—sweet mint and elderflower along with a zingy hint of that lime—was begging to be made into a snackable treat.

Feel free to get creative if you prefer orange, lemon, or grapefruit; swap out the elderflower for maraschino liqueur or sambuca; or give fresh basil or even sage a turn in place of mint.

Makes 20 to 25 cookies

1¾ cups (210 g) all-purpose flour (or rice flour if you prefer gluten-free)

1 teaspoon (5 g) baking soda

1 teaspoon (3 g) kosher salt

½ cup (115 g) unsalted butter, softened

¾ cup (150 g) granulated sugar

Grated zest and juice of 1 lime

1 large egg

1 tablespoon (15 mL) St-Germain liqueur

OPTIONAL GLAZE

1 cup (120 g) powdered sugar

Grated zest and juice of 1 lime

Chopped fresh mint, for garnish (optional)

In a medium bowl, sift together the flour, baking soda, and salt. In a separate medium bowl (or the bowl of a stand mixer), cream together the butter, granulated sugar, and lime zest. It's easiest to use a handheld electric or stand mixer, if available, but you can also use a wooden spoon and mix by hand. Once creamy, add the egg and whisk, then the lime juice and liqueur. The batter will have a fluffy texture and may look a bit "curdled," but will become smooth when the flour is folded in. Using a rubber spatula, gradually incorporate the flour mixture and knead into a soft dough by hand. Cover and rest in the refrigerator for about 30 minutes. The dough will be sticky; if you're working in a high humidity environment, chill for a bit longer until the dough is easier to handle.

Preheat the oven to 350°F / 175°C. Line a sheet pan with Silpat or parchment paper.

Remove the dough from the refrigerator and, using a cookie dropper or forming by hand, make 20 to 25 roughly golf ball–size portions. Arrange on the lined sheet pan, allowing about an inch between cookies, and flatten slightly by hand. Bake for 12 to 15 minutes, until slightly golden around the edges and set in the center. (The bake time will vary a bit depending on how long you chill the dough.) Let cool.

MAKE THE GLAZE

Mix the powdered sugar with enough lime juice to make it slightly thinner than a paste.

Spread the glaze over the cooled cookies. Garnish with lime zest or chopped mint as the glaze sets if you like.

note If using additional lime zest for garnish, it helps to zest in advance of decorating and allow the zest to dry a bit. This will make fast sprinkling easier and prevent clumping! You can also sub out some of the lime juice for more St-Germain if you'd like a boozier, more elderflower-forward glaze.

Giuggiulena
Sicilian Sesame Brittle

VEGETARIAN, GF

The cuisine of Sicily reflects heavy and wide-ranging influences thanks to a long history of conquest by a variety of cultures, including a period when the island was an Islamic emirate. That era concluded in the eleventh century, yet evidence lingers in the form of ingredients like raisins and pine nuts, cinnamon and saffron, as well as sesame seeds.

In dialect, these flavorful little flecks have a smattering of fun-to-say names, including giuggiulena, gigiolena, giuggiulena, and ciciulena. And while sesame seeds are found in everything from breads to pastas, my personal favorite appearance is in the form of these crunchy, sticky bites that are typically a holiday treat—but in my opinion work for all occasions. Because they straddle the line between savory and sweet, they pair extremely well with bitter aperitivo cocktails, despite "technically" being a dessert.

If you care to tinker with the traditional, you can swap in your choice of nuts and seeds, even exchange honey for maple syrup, or try a spicy, hot honey instead of orange blossom.

Makes 18 to 20 (2-inch) pieces

⅓ cup (100 mL) honey, preferably orange blossom

¼ cup (50 g) granulated sugar

1 cup (about 125 g) sesame seeds (white, or a mixture of white and black), toasted

1 cup (100 g) almonds, toasted and chopped

Grated zest of 1 orange

Flake sea salt, q.b.

Line a flat surface or sheet pan with Silpat or parchment.

In a medium heavy-bottomed saucepan, heat the honey and sugar over low heat, stirring occasionally, until the sugar is dissolved. Add the sesame seeds and almonds and cook until the mixture is golden brown, 15 to 20 minutes. Remove from the heat, stir in the zest, and pour onto the parchment/Silpat. Working quickly, use a lightly oiled rolling pin to spread the mixture evenly to about ¼ inch thick. Use a sharp knife to cut into strips or a diamond pattern and sprinkle with sea salt.

Allow to cool completely, then break up into pieces along the cut lines and serve. Store any remaining brittle in an airtight container for up to 2 weeks.

Seada di Sarda
Sardinian Turnovers

Seada, a fritter traditional to the island of Sardinia, has a lot in common with a Spanish empanada. This could be pure coincidence, or perhaps the 300-year period during which Spain had control of the island resulted in some parallel culinary thinking.

Either way, seada is usually considered a dessert dish these days, sometimes served with a dusting of powdered sugar. But the complexity that comes from the savory, rich lardo and the salty pecorino sardo (a young, fresh type of sheep's milk cheese) combined with a drizzle of sweet honey and a burst of bright lemon zest is satisfying at any time of day—and is a perfect complement to many bitter classic aperitivo drinks.

If you aren't able to source pecorino sardo, you can substitute another soft sheep's milk cheese. Fresh Asiago and Gruyère, while not traditional, are also good options.

Makes 6 servings

1½ cups (244 g) semolina flour

½ cup (125 mL) warm water

Kosher salt, q.b.

2 tablespoons (28 g) lardo

2 cups (225 g) shredded pecorino sardo (fresh young pecorino)

Grated zest of 1 lemon, plus more for garnish

Peanut oil, q.b.

Honey, q.b.

In a medium mixing bowl or the bowl of a stand mixer, combine the flour and warm water with salt and mix (by hand or in the mixer with a paddle attachment). Gradually incorporate the lardo and knead until smooth. Once a dough forms, cover with plastic and let rest for about 30 minutes.

Line a sheet pan with Silpat or parchment and set aside.

In a medium pot over medium heat, melt the cheese, stirring regularly to prevent burning. You may need a splash of water to kickstart the melting process, or a touch of flour if you have trouble keeping it together. Once fully melted, fold in the lemon zest and pour onto the lined sheet, spreading with a rubber or offset spatula until it's about ¼ inch thick. Allow to fully cool. Use 2½-inch biscuit or cookie cutters to cut out six rounds; set aside.

Meanwhile, roll the dough onto a lightly floured surface to about ⅛ inch thick. Use 4-inch cookie or biscuit cutters to cut out twelve rounds.

Place one piece of the cheese filling on top of one dough round, then cover with another dough round. Use a fork to close each. They will look like hand pies, or large ravioli.

Heat about ¾ inch peanut oil in a heavy-bottomed frying pan to about 340°F / 170°C. In batches, add the pastries and fry until golden brown on the bottom. Turn gently and repeat on the other side. Drain on paper towels.

Serve with a generous drizzle of honey and more citrus zest.

notes You can also bake the seada at 375°F / 190°C for 12 to 15 minutes, if preferred.

Some cooks will forgo the cheese melting step, choosing instead to simply place a small pile of cheese and lemon zest directly into the dough pockets. This may result in a slightly less consistent filling.

Chiacchierare

Aperitivo is perfect for catching up with friends and having *una piccola chiacchierata*, literally, "a little chat." And when chatting with anyone in Italy, there's a 99 percent chance* you'll be talking about food.

In the event that you're *not* talking about food, you're probably still going to be using food as a metaphor, so here are a few handy food-related idioms that you might come across, or may just decide to sprinkle into conversation yourself.

*This is technically an untested number, but a very probable, educated guess based on experience.

PHRASE	TRANSLATION	MEANING AND EXPLANATION
Acqua in bocca!	Water in the mouth!	An exclamation urging someone to keep a secret (because to open one's mouth when it is full of water would be to "spill")
Andare a tutta birra	To get all the beer	To go very fast; to run at full speed Historically, horses were given beer as a source of energy, and to get all the beer meant to go at full speed.
Come il cavolo a merenda	Like cauliflower for a snack	A description of something illogical, crazy, that makes no sense
Prendersi uno spaghetto. **Mi sono preso uno spaghetto.**	I got myself one spaghetto.	To receive a shock. Because what on earth does one do with *uno spaghetto* (a single strand of spaghetti)?!
Molto fumo e poco arrosto	A lot of smoke, but very little roast	Someone is "all talk," or something is of very little substance.
Non tutte le ciambelle escono col buco.	Not all the doughnuts have a hole.	Not everything is perfect, but even a doughnut without a hole can be delicious.
Se non è zuppa è pan bagnato.	If it's not soup, it's wet bread.	Six of one, half dozen of the other This refers to Tuscan culinary traditions of *ribollita* (a soup made with leftover bread) or *panzanella* (a salad made with leftover bread). You may have leftover bread, but you can't have both the salad and the soup (especially as these are distinctly winter and summer dishes, respectively).
Dire pane al pane e vino al vino.	Say bread for bread and wine for wine.	Call it like it is.

8

COCKTAILS

Italian cocktail culture is a particular style of mixology. Like the country's cooking, it is often simple, with few ingredients and clean, equal parts ratios (or, in the case of the Classic Spritz, as easy as 1, 2, 3). The following is a selection of stalwart sippers, along with some suggested variations. As we have seen, thanks to creative mixologists all over the world, these drinks are easy frameworks that invite experimentation, and—much like everything else in Italian eating and drinking—they respect, appreciate, and even demand that seasonality and regionality be taken into account. (Note: Unless otherwise indicated, each cocktail recipe makes one cocktail.)

Garibaldi

This drink is everything I love about Italian food and drink culture. It could not be simpler with its two-ingredient composition, and yet it manages to also be a profound story in a glass. Allegedly, it was created to demonstrate unity in Italian culture: Campari is a northern product, and oranges are native to the south. Giuseppe Garibaldi, a general remembered for his contribution to Italian unification in 1871, is the namesake for this drink—a metaphor for the country finally coming together.

The key to the recipe is all in the orange juice, which is usually described as "fluffy" in a Garibaldi. Instead of simply mixing the drink screwdriver-style, there is added flair with fluffing—a technique intended to highlight and pay proper respect to the precious citrus. There are a few ways to achieve this texture. You can either whip by hand with a whisk, pulse quickly in a blender or with an immersion blender, or use a hand frother (the kind commonly sold for making at-home cappuccino).

1½ ounces (45 mL) Campari

4 ounces (120 mL) "fluffy" orange juice

½ orange wheel

Fill a highball or wine glass with ice, then add the Campari. Top with the fluffy juice and garnish with half an orange wheel.

VARIATION

Pineapple Garibaldi

1½ ounces (45 mL) Luxardo Bitter Bianco
4 ounces (120 mL) "fluffy" pineapple juice
Pineapple wedge

Fill a highball or wine glass with ice, then add the Bitter Bianco. Top with the fluffy juice and garnish with the pineapple wedge.

According to some sources, including beverage industry news source *Drinks International,* the Negroni is now the most-ordered drink in the world. Its devotees are legion, its interpretations seemingly limitless, its history endlessly quotable—allegedly created for Count Camillo Negroni in 1919, when a Florentine bar obliged his request to swap in gin for the soda water in an Americano—and its appeal showing no signs of slowing.

But how is it that a cocktail more than a century old has become a global phenomenon in just the last few years? It's likely a confluence of factors, social and economic, both global and local to Italy:

SIMPLICITY

To make a Negroni, one does not need a mixology course, nor a deeply stocked bar. One part Campari (or other bitter aperitivo), one part gin, one part vermouth. This simple, batch-able composition makes it ideal for entertaining, too, and in the last decade the alcohol industry has taken note. The RTD (ready-to-drink) category is filled with brands that have already mixed your next Negroni, like Brooklyn's St. Agrestis.

AESTHETICS

It was Apicius—an ancient Roman noble and namesake of what is considered one of the first recipe collections—who coined the adage "Il cibo si mangia prima con gli occhi." (Food is eaten first with the eyes.) The ruby red bitters, cut crystal tumblers, and iconic orange slice of the Negroni resonate online a lot more effectively than a glass of wine or a beer, elevating its image to iconic.

ADAPTABILITY

An undeniable appeal of the Negroni is its endless adaptability; one can quickly count classic, easy-to-mix variations, including the Americano, sbagliato, and Milano Torino (my personal favorite). But within the blueprint of the original recipe, it's also easy to infuse any of the ingredients (or several), swap out vermouth or gin choices, and experiment with different bitter liqueurs and garnishes.

FLAVOR

The Negroni's simplicity is deceiving when you consider the complexity of its flavor profile: Perfectly balanced bitter and sweet, it is a study in agrodolce. And the rise of the Negroni also likely has to do with a shift in the public palate. Kale, dark chocolate, chicories, and black coffee have all become major elements of today's culinary zeitgeist, making palates primed and ready for this cocktail's grand comeback.

Whatever factors created this new stage for the Negroni, few are complaining, and it's not just the Campari Group swerving its biciclette all the way to the bank. Craft distillers on both sides of the Atlantic have their own versions of Negroni ingredients and RTDs. Thanks to old Count Negroni, countless jobs have been created, glasses lifted, and moments marked by this enduring classic.

Negroni

What can one say about the Negroni that hasn't been said? Anthony Bourdain, Stanley Tucci, and even Ernest Hemingway are all famed for their love of Count Negroni's namesake—a drink whose fiery appearance reflects the deep passion of its followers.

In some ways, what is so compelling about this drink is exactly what appeals to so many people about Italian food and beverage in general: the commitment to good quality ingredients with minimal fussiness or complication, leading to nothing more than pure satisfaction.

1 ounce (30 mL) dry gin

1 ounce (30 mL) vermouth (like Cinzano Rosso or Punt e Mes)

1 ounce (30 mL) Campari

½ orange wheel or 1 orange twist

Combine the gin, vermouth, and Campari in a mixing glass with ice and stir until well-chilled. Strain into an old-fashioned or rocks glass with ice and garnish with orange.

CLASSIC NEGRONI VARIATIONS

Italians are famous for taking a preparation, changing a single element, and rebranding the entire thing (think: cacio e pepe, carbonara, and alla gricia pastas in the Roman canon).

The Americano is essentially the Negroni, minus the gin and with a splash of soda water. It's the low ABV version for those looking for something lighter.

Despite having a name that translates into English as "mistaken," in my mind, the Negroni sbagliato can do no wrong. Though the intentionality is still debated, legend has it that back in the 1970s, a Milan-based bartender in the process of making a classic Negroni accidentally poured Prosecco instead of gin. The result is a delicious take that's slightly less alcoholic than the Negroni and more of a cousin of the spritz, balanced and bitter and bubbly. If that's doing something wrong, I don't want to be right.

The bergamotto variation is a white Negroni, with the bitter Campari element replaced with Italicus, and the red vermouth with a dry white. The floral notes of the liqueur and the gin botanicals really shine, and I love this particular cocktail in spring and summer paired with herbaceous stuzzichini.

Americano

1½ ounces (45 mL) Campari

1½ ounces (45 mL) vermouth (like Cinzano Rosso or Punt e Mes)

Soda water, q.b.

½ orange wheel or 1 orange twist

Combine the Campari and vermouth in a highball glass with ice. Top with soda water and stir gently. Garnish with orange.

(CONTINUES)

Sbagliato

1 ounce (30 mL) Campari

1 ounce (30 mL) vermouth (like Cinzano Rosso or
    Punt e Mes)

1 ounce (30 mL) Prosecco

½ orange wheel or 1 orange twist

In a rocks, highball, or red wine glass, or a champagne
flute, combine the Campari and vermouth with ice.
Top with the Prosecco and stir gently. Garnish
with orange.

note The sbagliato ratio is a suggestion. Some bartenders
use more Prosecco or prefer a slightly sweeter drink made by
increasing the ratio of vermouth to Campari.

Bergamotto Negroni

1 ounce (30 mL) dry gin

1 ounce (30 mL) dry white vermouth

1 ounce (30 mL) Italicus liqueur (or similar rosolio)

Olive

Combine the gin, vermouth, and liqueur in a cocktail
shaker with ice and stir well, until very cold. Strain into
an old-fashioned or rocks glass, serve over ice, and
garnish with a briny olive.

Pro-Ginepro

Gin may be a decidedly British spirit, with common origin stories crediting the U.K. and Holland for its invention, but Italians have a claim to stake, too. That's thanks to fragrant juniper, gin's most iconic ingredient, which is historically abundant in parts of the peninsula. In Salerno, for example, Benedictine monks used the berries to infuse neutral-flavored alcoholic tonics as far back as the sixteenth century. There's even speculation that the name itself is a derivative of the Italian word for juniper—*ginepro*.

While today the more common associations with gin may be with Spain's complex and flamboyant gin-tonics, or the classic martini with its American roots, a significant number of major gin brands around the world still use Italian juniper. Tishanah Welcome, operations manager for Peter in Florence—a small producer in Tuscany—says that *Juniperus communis,* which is native to Tuscany, is considered "one of the best because of the fragrant, herbal aroma with notes of pine, camphor, and lavender."

Tishanah explains the importance of gin and juniper to the Italian economy and identity: "Some of the biggest selling gin brands worldwide source juniper from Tuscany; it is said that 47 percent of juniper used to produce gin comes from Tuscany."

She tells me that the gin industry has grown exponentially in the last four or five years, and that this popularity is an opportunity to educate consumers, particularly about the origins of the ingredients.

"Most important to the Tuscan economy is the identity," she says. She compares the effort to assert this identity with the Made in Italy brand, but with a hyperspecificity common to other Italian products (prosciutto di Parma, balsamic vinegar of Modena, etc.). Tishanah emphasizes that Peter in Florence's gin is not only made in Italy, not only in Tuscany, but in Chianti, explaining that the main ingredients—including the Tuscan juniper and iris flowers—are specific to the Chianti hills.

Today, the popularity of the Negroni and its cousins has helped open the door for the nation at large to reclaim its connection to the base spirit—as well as economic opportunities for modern, creative distillers and storytellers. Gin brands like Malfy, Portofino, and Ginarte also utilize Italian juniper in addition to other locally grown and indigenous ingredients, all in an attempt to cement the country's long-standing connection to a spirit that powers so many cocktails around the world.

Milano Torino

The classic Milano Torino is a celebration of the Italian north, and the recipe is right in the name if you read between the lines. Milano is a reference to one of the city's proudest products (Campari) and Torino nods to vermouth di Torino.

It is a straight-to-the-point kind of drink in both name and composition. To me, it is the absolute perfect aperitivo drink that combines the appetite opening qualities of both vermouth and bitters, without the alcoholic heft of a Negroni.

1 ounce (30 mL) Campari

1 ounce (30 mL) vermouth

Orange twist

Place 1 large ice cube in an old-fashioned or rocks glass. Add the Campari and vermouth and stir. Garnish with an orange twist.

VARIATION

Rosemary Pinoli Mi-To

1 ounce (30 mL) pinoli-infused Campari
(see Note)

1 ounce (30 mL) vermouth

1 sprig fresh rosemary

Place 1 large ice cube in an old-fashioned or rocks glass. Add the Campari and vermouth and stir. Garnish with rosemary.

note For the infused Campari, steep 2 sprigs fresh rosemary and 1 tablespoon toasted pine nuts in 1 cup Campari for 24 to 48 hours. Strain and store in an airtight glass jar. You can keep it for about a month, but it probably won't be around that long. (For more infusion suggestions, see page 230.)

Boulevardier

As a whiskey drinker in Italy, I don't always find my favorite cocktails on the menu, as the brown spirit isn't a commonly consumed one. Thankfully, the Boulevardier—a twist on the Negroni that substitutes whiskey for the gin—has been my saving grace.

Perhaps it should be no surprise that this drink was allegedly created for another, far more notable American expatriate and writer than myself, this one of the 1920s—Erskine Gwynne. As the story goes, it was developed in Paris, where Gwynne was the editor of a publication called *The Boulevardier.*

I've often heard it referred to as a cold weather companion to the Negroni, but personally I love this drink all year long.

1 ounce (30 mL) whiskey, preferably bourbon or rye

1 ounce (30 mL) Campari

1 ounce (30 mL) sweet vermouth

Orange twist

Combine the whiskey, Campari, and vermouth in a mixing glass with ice. Mix well, until thoroughly chilled. Strain into a martini or coupe glass and garnish with an orange twist for an "up" version. Or for a classic on-the-rocks version, use an old-fashioned glass with a large ice cube.

VARIATION

Chocolate Boulevardier

The Boulevardier is delicious with a chocolate infusion: Simply add about 10 g cacao nibs to 12 ounces (about ½ bottle) of Campari. Allow to steep overnight (or longer for more intense results). Strain out the nibs and proceed with the cocktail preparation. Serve in an old-fashioned or rocks glass, or serve up in a coupe or martini glass. (For more infusion suggestions, see page 230.)

Boulevards of New England

A great many drinks in Italy tell a story about the places they originated from or the characters who were the inspiration. As a child of an Italian American community, raised in New England, I considered the elements that might be mixed up in a tale of my own place.

I adore a Negroni, but my base spirit of choice is always whiskey, and after having a cocktail made with a thickened balsamic vinegar one evening in Florence, I realized that my own neck of the woods produces something viscous, sweet, and evocative as well—maple syrup. A bit of tart northeastern fruit comes into play with the cranberries, and a few drops of saline solution balance the whole affair. The drink may have very New England elements, but the philosophy of distilling a place into something that can be shared is entirely Italian.

1 ounce (30 mL) Campari

3 to 5 fresh cranberries

1 ounce (30 mL) spiced vermouth (I like to infuse a classic like Punt e Mes with cinnamon sticks, anise pods, whole cloves, vanilla bean, and orange peel, but you can get creative based on your preference)

1 ounce (30 mL) whiskey

½ ounce (15 mL) maple syrup (see Note)

2 drops saline solution (recipe below)

Candied cranberries, for garnish (optional)

Orange twist

Combine the Campari and cranberries in a cocktail shaker and muddle. Add the vermouth, whiskey, maple syrup, and saline, then ice, and stir vigorously until well-chilled.

Strain the drink into a rocks or old-fashioned glass with one large ice cube, or serve up in a coupe if you prefer your boulevardier-style drinks neat. Garnish with candied cranberries if you have them, and an orange twist.

note As a northeasterner and an Italian obsessed with quality, natural ingredients, I feel strongly that finding and investing in real maple syrup is a must (for this recipe, and as a life general principle), as many grocery store brands are maple-flavored corn syrups with not a drop of the actual precious sap to be found. I love Tree Juice syrup from New York, which ships nationally, but there are a ton of great farms in the Northeast that will happily accommodate.

SALINE SOLUTION

Makes ¼ cup

Boil 3½ teaspoons (20 g) table salt with about ¼ cup (about 60 mL) water, until the salt dissolves. Allow the solution to cool completely. This amount should last you a good long time since you'll only use a drop or two for this drink, but it is incredibly useful stuff.

I like to store half in a dropper bottle for drinks, and the other in a spray bottle for dressing food. Give a spritz of this stuff to corn on the cob or just about anything to which you'd want to add salt (which is everything). It is the only way to apply salt to popcorn or homemade potato chips, as far as I'm concerned.

Classic Spritz

Much has been made of the history and invention of the Classic Spritz, but with its present popularity, whether or not the drink has a bright future is a lot less debatable.

Aperol has taken the liberty of publishing the basic 3-2-1 recipe on its bottle (and nearly every other surface with which a drinker might interact), but in case you need a refresher on one of the world's most refreshing drinks, the formula is as follows—though, like many of the recipes in this book, it's open to many interpretations. See below for some suggestions and inspiration.

3 ounces (90 mL) Prosecco

2 ounces (60 mL) Aperol or Campari

1 ounce (30 mL) soda water

In a wine glass filled with ice, combine all the ingredients and stir gently. While a wine glass is classic, you can use anything from a simple highball to a more elaborate goblet—whatever fits your spritz style in the moment.

SPRITZ IT UP: BITTERSWEET INSPIRATION

The spritz formula makes an ideal blueprint to get inventive and tell a tale with your cocktail. Here are just a few ideas to get the creative juicing sparkling.

SWAP OUT THE SODA WATER FOR:
* Sanpellegrino Limonata or Aranciata
* Flavored kombucha
* Juice, like citrus, pineapple, or passion fruit (I've even seen carrot and celery juice spritzes), either in place of the soda water entirely, or as a split, depending on your taste

SWAP OUT THE PROSECCO FOR:
* Sparkling rosé
* Lambrusco
* Sparkling cider
* Sake
* Ginger beer
* Beer (Use a hefeweizen and substitute 1 ounce lemon juice for soda water to make a drink called an Aperol Mist; or try a fruity sour beer for something tart and totally new.)

SWAP THE BASE SPIRIT FOR:
* An infused Aperol, Campari, or your preferred base bitter (see infusion table on page 230)
* Alternate bitters from Luxardo, Select, Contratto, or Cappelletti; or stateside interpretations from St. George, Lo-Fi, St. Agrestis, or Leopold Bros. (to name just a few!)
* An herbaceous amaro, like Vecchio Amaro del Capo, Amaro Montenegro, or Cynar; or a liqueur like limoncello
* Suze, Lillet, Italicus, or similar for a different dimension, flavorwise

GARNISH OR ADD FLAIR OR A BOOZY BOOST:
* Add fresh herbs like sage, rosemary, or thyme.
* Drop in briny olives or capers, candied citrus peel (page 200) or ginger, or pickled fruit (page 94).
* Fortify with a shot of a stronger spirit like gin, brandy, grappa, or whiskey.
* Bring depth with a few dashes of bitters or a simple syrup, saline solution, or vinegary shrub.

Infusions

Infusions are such a fun way to play with a cocktail's flavor profile. Here are just a few ideas and ratios.

When infusing, make sure you clean the ingredients first, then combine in a mason jar or other airtight container. Store in a cool, dark place, and shake your jar or bottle occasionally throughout the steeping period.

The length of time you'll want to infuse will depend on your desired intensity and the strength of the ingredient's flavor (for example, hot peppers will infuse faster than figs). I recommend tasting regularly to keep track of the progress. When the flavor passes your taste test, strain the spirit through a cheesecloth or fine-mesh strainer and return to an airtight container in a cool, dark place. While alcohol infusions can potentially last for years at room temperature and sediment is natural, adding produce and fresh ingredients can introduce the possibility of off flavors and mold developing over time. I usually abide by a 3-month shelf life as a general rule.

INFUSION INGREDIENT	SUGGESTED SPIRITS	AMOUNT FOR 750 ML SPIRITS	TIME	SUGGESTED DRINK
Vanilla bean	Any	2 vanilla beans, split lengthwise	2 to 4 weeks	Vanilla Bicerin: Substitute infused grappa in the Bicerin recipe (page 241).
Coffee or chocolate	Vodka, gin, Campari	½ cup whole coffee beans or cacao nibs	Overnight or up to about 1 week	Coffee Americano: Substitute infused Campari or whiskey in the Americano recipe (page 221).
Peach and basil (or other fruit and herb)	Gin, whiskey, Campari, Aperol	1 peach, halved and pitted 1 handful fresh basil leaves	About 2 weeks	Peach Basil Bicicletta: Substitute infused Campari in the Bicicletta recipe (page 236).
Tomato	Gin, vodka, Campari	1 pound (450 g) cherry or grape tomatoes, halved	About 1 week	Tomato Negroni: Substitute infused Campari or gin in the Negroni recipe (page 221).
Hot peppers (in Italy, I use a tiny variety of dried red peppers, but jalapeño, serrano, and habanero all work well)	Gin, whiskey, grappa, Campari, Aperol, tequila, amaro	4 ounces (115 g) or about 4 jalapeños, thinly sliced (seeds removed if you prefer a milder heat)	Overnight, or up to about 3 days	Spicy Sbagliato: Substitute infused Campari in the Sbagliato variation (page 222).
Fig and cardamom (or other dried fruit and spice)	Gin, whiskey, grappa, Aperol	2 cardamom pods 1 cup (150 g) dried figs, halved	About 2 weeks	Fig Cardamom Americano: Substitute infused gin or Campari in the Americano variation (page 221).
Coconut	Campari, gin, tequila, grappa, Aperol	1 cup (100 g) unsweetened coconut flakes (toasted in the oven for about 10 minutes at 350°F / 175°C)	3 days to 1 week	Coconut Spritz: Substitute infused Aperol in the Classic Spritz recipe (page 229).
Nuts (hazelnuts, almonds, walnuts, pecans, all work especially well; be wary of nuts that are more oily, like cashews, peanuts, and pine nuts)	Any	1½ cups (130 g) nuts (shelled and/or peeled and toasted in the oven for about 15 minutes at 350°F / 175°C)	1 to 2 weeks	Nutty Grappa Manhattan: Substitute infused grappa in the Aged Grappa Manhattan recipe (page 244). I highly recommend hazelnuts here.

Green Spritz

The Green Spritz is another example of aesthetics as aperitivo inspiration. It's a little less common to find around the country, because the base ingredient—a liqueur called P31—is relatively new. Conceived in 2017 in Padua, the eye-catching spirit has inspired a whole lot of pointing by bar-goers curious to know what their neighbors are drinking.

While the color and flavor are reminiscent of absinthe (both count wormwood as an ingredient), the low-ish alcohol content makes it a natural fit for the breezy spritz formula.

3 ounces (90 mL) Prosecco

2 ounces (60 mL) P31 Green Aperitivo (see Notes)

1 ounce (30 mL) soda water

¼ ounce (8 mL) lime juice

Lime wedge

In a wine glass filled with ice, combine the Prosecco, P31, soda water, and lime juice and stir gently. Garnish with a lime wedge.

notes If you can't get your hands on P31, you can also make a fun and festive, fruity and sweet, Green Spritz with Midori, which is more widely available.

Also, if you *do* get your hands on P31, you can also try their recipe for a green Negroni, which calls for equal parts P31, white vermouth, and gin, with a lime twist.

Hugo Spritz

Despite being relatively unknown in North America, the Hugo is well traveled throughout its home country—not to mention parts of Germany and Austria. By most accounts, it is a relatively young addition to the aperitivo canon, added in 2005 when a bartender in South Tyrol decided to create an alternative spritz to the Venetian style.

The Hugo might look like a mojito, with its mint and lime garnishes, but the flavor profile is distinctly Italian. The elderflower plant, or *fior di sambuco,* grows widely across Alpine regions of Europe. Originally the drink was created with an elderflower syrup, but the increased availability of elderflower liqueurs like the French-made St-Germain (born in 2007) likely contributed to the proliferation of the Hugo, as making the drink no longer required the mixologist to do the work of making their own syrup.

Search the internet and you will find a *lot* of formulas for this drink. Some call for as little as ½ ounce of elderflower liqueur, while others recommend up to 2 ounces. Some suggest 2 ounces of Prosecco and 2 ounces of soda water, and some call for as much as 5 ounces of the latter, or a splash of gin. In terms of method, you might see the mint and/or citrus muddled, or simply added as a garnish.

Italian bartenders around the country have similarly disparate opinions, so this is my personal favorite preparation, as I prefer a drier version with unmuddled garnishes, but feel free to play with the recipe until you come upon your Hugo, come vuoi.

2 ounces (60 mL) Prosecco

¾ ounce (22 mL) St-Germain or Fiorento elderberry liqueur

2 ounces (60 mL) soda water

Fresh mint leaves

Lime wedge

Fill a wine glass about three-fourths full with ice. Add the Prosecco and St-Germain, then top with soda water. Garnish with mint and a wedge of lime.

VARIATION

Basil Grapefruit Hugo

¾ ounce (22 mL) St-Germain liqueur
2 ounces (60 mL) Prosecco
2 ounces (60 mL) soda water
2 to 3 fresh basil leaves
Grapefruit wedge

Fill a wine glass about three-fourths full with ice. Add the St-Germain and Prosecco, then top with soda water. Garnish with basil and a wedge of grapefruit.

Rosolio

APERITIVO DI CORTE, IN THE MODERN COCKTAIL BAR

Supposedly introduced by the Arabs sometime around the fifteenth century, produced by Tuscan and Sicilian nuns for a few hundred years, beloved by the Medici family, and pronounced the "Aperitivo di Corte" by the King of Savoy in the eighteenth century, rosolio is still referred to by its cult followers as "the original aperitivo."

Over the years, rosolio variations have been infused with *cedro* (cedar), cinnamon, and fennel, but the basic framework (sugar, alcohol, and water) invites adaptation, and has varied widely from region to region.

And still, despite its proliferation, adaptability, and one-time popularity, this spirit disappeared almost entirely from the canon of consumables in the late 1700s, thanks to a push toward focusing on vermouth by King Vittorio Amedeo III.

Fortunately, today's creative cocktail professionals have been digging around for inspiration, and have given distillers good reason to bring back this storied spirit. In particular, Italicus—launched in 2016—has found purchase in the market, building its flavor profile upon the essential oils of UNESCO-protected Calabrian bergamot, as well as chamomile, lavender, gentian, yellow roses, and melissa flowers, ingredients sourced from all over the peninsula in an effort to represent the vast Italian bounty.

The name *rosolio* is derived from the Latin *ros solis*, or "dew of the sun," and today the category is diverse and ripe for innovation. Distillers from Sicily to Turin have been experimenting and producing, and spirits enthusiasts eagerly await the next generation of this ancient drink.

Making your own rosolio is simple enough, and not unlike making the more well known Italian liqueur limoncello. But it does require a little patience. The recipe here is a framework. I substituted hibiscus for the more traditional rose petals, which adds tartness and a regal purple hue, and added fresh ginger for a little kick.

Rosolio di Zenzero di Ibisco
Hibiscus Ginger Rosolio

Makes about 1 quart

1 to 1¼ cups (40 to 50 g) dried hibiscus flowers

1 vanilla bean, split

Peeled zest of 1 orange, cut into strips

2 anise pods

1 cinnamon stick

1 inch fresh ginger, peeled

2 cups (500 mL) grain alcohol

2 cups (500 mL) water

1½ cups (300 g) granulated sugar

In an airtight bottle or jar, combine the hibiscus, vanilla bean, orange zest, anise, cinnamon, and ginger with the alcohol. Store and leave in a cool, dark space for 10 to 14 days. Strain out the solids and return to the bottle.

In a medium saucepan, bring the water and sugar to a boil and simmer until reduced by about a third. Add the syrup to the infused alcohol and rest for another 2 weeks.

Enjoy chilled on its own, or as a cocktail ingredient (like in the following Hibiscus Ginger Spritz).

Hibiscus Ginger Spritz

¾ ounce (22 mL) Hibiscus Ginger Rosolio

3 ounces (90 mL) Prosecco

1 to 2 ounces (30 to 60 mL) soda water, q.b.

Candied ginger

Citrus wedge

Fill a wine glass about three-fourths full with ice. Add the rosolio and Prosecco, then top with soda water. Garnish with ginger and a wedge of citrus.

Bicicletta

The name of this classic Milanese cocktail is also a suggestion: Don't get behind the wheel of an automobile after one. The story goes that the moniker referred not to the suggested method of transportation itself, but to the men who couldn't keep their biciclette straight when they piloted them home post-aperitivo.

Today, this elegant drink appeals to imbibers of all persuasions, especially given its simple formula and adaptability. Swapping out soda water for sparkling limonata or flavored tonics can add dimension, and the selection of red bitters on the market can also serve to modify the cocktail's profile.

2 ounces (60 mL) dry white wine (like pinot grigio or Sauvignon blanc)

2 ounces (60 mL) Campari

Soda water, q.b. (see Note)

Citrus wheel

Combine the wine and Campari in a highball or wine glass and add ice. Top with soda water, stir gently, and garnish with an orange or lemon wheel.

note The amount of soda water in a bicicletta is another oft-debated and open-to-interpretation component of Italian cocktailing. Some say it should be a splash (about ½ ounce), while others have told me simply to "fill the rest of the glass" without ever specifying the size or type of glass. As with most "recipes" in the spritz family, how much water you want to add to your cocktail is adaptable to your mood and needs.

La Vita del Vino

WINE AND VERMOUTH ON THE STUZZICHINI TABLE

Vino is integral to Italian daily life, and that dedication extends to aperitivo hour as well. While cocktails tend to be favored as "appetite-opening" drinks, there's plenty of love for wine, too, and like everything in Italian culture, the curation is focused and intentional.

Certified wine specialist Dr. Danielle Callegari explains the characteristics of aperitivo-worthy wines, and the approach to their selection: "Italians are super attuned to the structure and body of the wine, its alcohol content, and how that interacts with your body and what you're consuming. Aperitivo is meant to be low in alcohol, [so] you might have something as low as 10 percent ABV [alcohol by volume] that is not, as they say in Italian, *impegnativo* [demanding]. [The wine is] meant to be juicy and light, so that you could have a full glass and not be worried about alcohol disrupting your ability to enjoy food or the rest of the evening."

Sparkling wine is a common sight paired with stuzzichini, as carbonation is considered to be an appetite stimulant. Danielle explains the wide variety of options beyond Prosecco, and their place in dining culture: "In Italy, sparklers are so critical to the narrative of a meal; different styles are conceived to play different roles." She describes the range, noting that there is "a great deal of difference between the Prosecco you would pop and adulterate with whatever bitter you have on hand," to create a spritz, and something like a Franciacorta, which, she says, is "made with a lot of intention, in the Champagne style and with an international market in mind."

Of course, there's always the part that wine plays in aperitivo cocktails, like the spritz (page 229) and bicicletta (page 236), but Danielle adds that "it would not be uncommon to mix [wine] with something, even juice or seltzer."

For a slightly different spin, fortified wine—namely vermouth—is another classic aperitivo, usually flavored with aromatics, botanicals, herbs, and spices. The northern Italian city of Turin in particular is credited as the birthplace of the Italian-style vermouth (usually sweet vermouth, as opposed to its drier French cousins). As the story goes, a man by the name of Antonio Benedetto Carpano crafted the first Italian vermouth in the northern city in 1786, which you may recognize as the brand Carpano Antica. Today, vermouth varieties are extensive, and my preferred bottle shop in Florence, Enoteca Alessi, boasts an entire wall ranging from classics (Carpano Antica, Cinzano, Martini & Rossi among them) to an abundance of modern takes and young producers from around the country and the world.

One of my latest favorites is a prime example of Italian tradition blended with innovation. The renowned Acetaia Giusti in Modena has been making prizewinning, world-famous balsamic vinegar for four centuries, and has now begun producing its own vermouth. The garnet liquid is a blend of red and white wines, aromatized with nineteen botanicals and a range of herbs and spices, including thyme, rosemary, lavender, black pepper, marjoram, nutmeg, and vanilla. Then it's spiked with saba (a sweet reduction of grape must) and aged in the company's legendary vinegar casks. The result is spectacular in a Negroni, yet equally sublime when sipped on its own. Take a stroll through your own neighborhood bottle shop to discover American vermouth makers that are adding to the aperitivo drink list, too.

At the end of the day, there's no wrong way to incorporate wine into your aperitivo practice, if, as Danielle reminds me, the idea is the same: "Anything to keep it light, and to wake up the palate."

Boozy Bicerin

Turin and the surrounding northern areas take coffee *very* seriously. But they also do chocolate exceptionally well, so it seems natural that this drink would emerge from the region. The bicerin takes Italy's famous *cioccolata calda* (hot chocolate) to another level, by adding espresso and whipped cream in a spectacular layered creation. The structured effect is possible because of the sheer weight of the chocolate component, which has a rich, luscious, pudding-like consistency, providing a sturdy base for the espresso and whipped cream.

Classically, bicerin is a nonalcoholic drink. However, I decided to take a *corretto* approach (a classic caffè corretto being an espresso "corrected" by adding a shot of liquor, usually grappa or sambuca). It may not be especially traditional, but I like to consider this boozy bicerin the Piemontese answer to the espresso martini.

(PICTURED OPPOSITE)

Makes 2 drinks

1 cup (250 mL) heavy cream

2 tablespoons (about 15 g) powdered sugar

1 cup (250 mL) whole milk

3 ounces (85 g) dark chocolate

2 ounces (60 mL) espresso

2 shots (about 90 mL) grappa

In a medium bowl (chilled to aid in whipping), whip the cream and powdered sugar until soft peaks form. In a small saucepan over low heat, combine the milk and chocolate and cook until the chocolate is melted and the mixture is thickened to a fudge-like consistency.

Layer the elements in a glass mug or footed goblet: first the chocolate, followed by the espresso and grappa, and finally top with the whipped cream.

Ponce Livornese

Consider this the working mariner's answer to the espresso martini. Born in the port city of Livorno on the coast of Tuscany, this after-meal drink is thought to have been developed as fortification for weary sailors as far back as the seventeenth century.

Naturally, there's a legend to this Livornese specialty that swirls around, involving a few barrels of rum breaking open in the cargo hold of a transatlantic voyage and contaminating nearby coffee beans. Lo and behold, the flavor and effect were both very agreeable, and the lemon peel was plopped in the glass after being used to clean the rim. Other versions of the origin story include a twist on a spiked British tea made with lemon. You may hear the citrus peel referred to as *la vela* or "the sail" of the drink, and cinnamon is rumored to be added at times, but no matter how you spin it, the Ponce Livornese will guide you safely through a storm.

It's always a nice touch to preheat the glass before you serve. If you happen to have an espresso machine, steam the glass using its steam wand prior to filling. If you don't have an espresso machine, you can simply microwave the glass for about 15 seconds, or fill with hot water while you make the drink, then empty out the water and refill with your ponce.

1 teaspoon (5 g) granulated sugar

1 lemon twist

1 ounce (30 mL) spiced rum

1½ ounces (45 mL) freshly brewed espresso (about a shot)

Place the sugar and lemon twist in a shot glass or espresso cup, add the rum, top with the brewed espresso, and serve hot.

Bombardino

In northern and Alpine regions of Italy, even during the height of ski season, it is not uncommon to see congregations of Italians (and sport-seeking tourists) sitting outdoors, sipping icy spritzes. But if you, like me, tend to want something a bit more warming for your après-ski aperitivo, the Bombardino is for you. A cousin of eggnog, this drink is fortified with a stiff spirit of your choice and will give you plenty to look forward to between trips to the slopes—or in the comfort of your own home.

There's the easy way, and the less easy way of making this drink. If you happen to have a bottle of Zabov or Advocaat (traditional zabaglione egg liqueurs), you're a few steps ahead of the game. These are available in the U.S., though not widely. But never fear! I will show you how to make a Bombardino from scratch by making your own custard.

Of course, the rich drink could function as a meal all on its own, but for aperitivo purposes, pair with something salty and crisp like the Torta di Patate di Trentino (page 164), or something smoky and savory like Fagottini di Speck & Formaggio (page 49).

Makes 4 drinks

3 large egg yolks

2½ tablespoons (30 g) sugar

3 ounces (90 mL) brandy or whiskey

Whipped cream, q.b.

In a small metal bowl, whip the egg yolks and sugar until lightened in color and frothy with a whisk (you can do this by hand, or with the whisk attachment of an electric hand mixer).

On the stovetop, bring a small pot of water (about one-third full) to a simmer. Set the bowl with the egg mixture over the simmering water. Stir continuously with a rubber spatula until thickened; it should be custardy and similar to a rich eggnog. Remove from the heat.

Stir the whipped cream and brandy/whiskey into the custard, divide into four small glass mugs (I also like to use little jam jars), and top with more whipped cream.

Sgroppino al Limone

There is speculation that the word *sgroppino* is a derivative of the verb *sgrovigliare,* which means "to unravel" or "to untangle," or perhaps more appropriately in this case, "to unwind." What better way to relax than with vodka, Prosecco, and a scoop of sorbetto all in one glass?

    Traditionally this drink has been used as an *intermezzo,* or palate cleanser, or otherwise a *digestivo,* to loosen the palate or release flavors from a past course. That said, in recent years you may have seen this beautiful vodka lemon float on a brunch table, or at a beachfront bar on a hot summer day. You can eat it with a spoon if you're quick, but the sorbetto melts fast so it's more likely to be a sipper.

2 ounces (60 mL) Prosecco

½ ounce (15 mL) vodka

¼ to ½ cup (30 to 60 g or 1 healthy scoop) lemon sorbetto

Fresh mint or rosemary

Pour the Prosecco and vodka into a flute or wine glass. Add a scoop of sorbetto. Garnish with fresh herbs and enjoy!

Aged Grappa Manhattan

While whiskey isn't common in most parts of Italy, it is usually possible to find an aged grappa. When grappa is considered *barricata,* or matured in barrels, it takes on an amber hue that more closely resembles the brown spirit in both color and flavor, making it a natural stand-in for a cocktail like the classic Manhattan. (PICTURED OPPOSITE)

2 ounces (60 mL) aged grappa

1 ounce (30 mL) dry vermouth

2 dashes bitters

1 Sambuca-Poached Cherry (page 199)

Combine the grappa, vermouth, and bitters in a mixing glass with ice and stir well. Serve in a chilled martini or coupe glass garnished with a Sambuca cherry, or on the rocks.

note You can use un-aged grappa as well, but the aging process gives the cocktail a flavor profile more like a classic whiskey Manhattan.

Vin Brulé

Though this drink originated in colder, northern regions, take a stroll through most of Italy's major cities during the winter these days and you're likely to find locals and tourists alike roaming through the streets and holiday markets with a steaming cup of vin brulé.

A cousin of *glühwein,* or mulled wine, the spice and citrus profiles are easily adaptable to your preferences. Should you feel so inclined, a shot of rum, brandy, or grappa wouldn't be unwelcome, but whenever possible, serve with roasted chestnuts for the full Italian experience.

Makes 4 to 6 servings

1 (750 mL) bottle full-bodied red wine

1 cup (200 g) packed brown sugar

1 small apple, cored and cut into wedges

½ orange (plus peel for garnish)

½ lemon

2 pods star anise

2 sticks cinnamon, plus more for garnish

8 whole cloves, plus more for garnish

Pinch of freshly grated nutmeg, plus more for garnish

Combine all ingredients in a saucepan over medium-high heat, bring to a simmer, and simmer for about 10 minutes.

Ladle the liquid into glass mugs and garnish with orange peel, cinnamon sticks, cloves, and nutmeg, and serve hot.

Cocktail Analcolici
Nonalcoholic Cocktails

Given Italy's reputation for fine wine, liqueurs, and even beer, it might be hard to believe, but there are plenty of options available for those looking to opt out of alcohol (or for children, since they are welcome at aperitivo as well). Most bars and food service establishments offer small bitter sodas (in particular, the Sanbittèr brand in either red or white varieties); chinotto, which looks like cola but is actually derived from a type of orange and is on the bittersweet side; or limonati-style sparkling citrus drinks.

There are some parts of the world in which ordering a soda at a bar might be met with a bit of a scoff, and discerning patrons aren't always given the same treatment as their booze-imbibing buddies. But in Italy, order a mocktail or virgin bitter at aperitivo time, and it's not uncommon to receive your drink poured thoughtfully and with the same care, in a crystal glass, with a fresh garnish—and yes, even *con stuzzichini*.

The following recipes are dry takes on classic aperitivo cocktails, or inventions all their own.

Virgin Venetian

3 ounces (90 mL) orange juice

2 ounces (60 mL) nonalcoholic bitters (like Crodino or Sanbittèr Rosso)

1 ounce (30 mL) soda water

Olive

Orange wheel

In a wine glass or flute filled with ice, combine the orange juice, bitters, and soda water and stir gently. Garnish with an olive and orange wheel.

Not-Limoncello Spritz

2 ounces (60 mL) freshly squeezed lemon juice

¾ ounce (22 mL) honey

4 ounces (120 mL) soda water

Fresh mint leaf

Fill a wine glass about three-fourths full with ice. In a cocktail shaker, shake the lemon juice and honey together with ice. Strain into the glass, then top with soda water and garnish with mint.

Luxardo Cherry Vanilla Cream Soda

1 ounce (30 mL) cherry syrup (from the Luxardo cherry jar)

½ ounce (15 mL) half and half

Seeds from ½ vanilla bean (or 1½ teaspoons vanilla extract)

3½ ounces (100 mL) soda water

Mix together the syrup, half and half, and vanilla in a mixing glass. Strain into a milkshake glass or tumbler over ice. Top with soda water and serve.

Blueberry Balsamic Shrub Soda

2 cups (340 g) blueberries

1 cup (200 g) granulated sugar

½ cup (150 mL) honey

1½ cups (350 mL) balsamic vinegar

½ cup (125 mL) apple cider vinegar

Soda water

Thyme sprig

Place the blueberries in a bowl with the sugar and honey and muddle gently. Add both vinegars, cover the bowl with plastic, and refrigerate for at least 2 days. The longer it infuses, the better. A week or two is a great amount of time.

Remove from the fridge and strain out the blueberries through a fine mesh sieve, pressing to extract as much shrub as possible. Makes about 2 cups. Store in an airtight jar or bottle in the refrigerator for up to 6 months.

To make one cocktail, combine 1 ounce shrub with 3½ to 4 ounces soda water (or to taste). Mix and serve over ice in a highball glass, garnished with a sprig of thyme.

If you care for a non-virgin, spritz-like cocktail, split the soda water with Prosecco: 1 ounce shrub, 2 ounces Prosecco, and 2 ounces soda water (or to taste.)

Conscientious Cocktailing at the Bar and in the Home

There is so much to enjoy and appreciate about aperitivo. For patrons, it's a chance to unwind, connect with friends, and try some new foods. For the country's culture and economy, the global popularity of aperitivo can bring new opportunities to Italians. That could be directly in food and beverage as a producer, farmer, or an entrepreneur; in marketing, advertising, and communications; or in crafts like blowing glassware or pouring candles to sit on bar tables—even making neon signs (see page 168). Italians are a proud people under any circumstance. With the popularity of this custom, they can harness that pride and inspiration and share even more of their culture with a captive audience of visitors.

Italy, though, like the rest of the world, also experiences some deleterious effects of tourism and cultural exchange. Being a conscientious participant—on both sides of the Atlantic—helps preserve the art and culture and ensure that these customs can survive for future visitors. When hosting an aperitivo at home, those same principles are important to keep in mind when entertaining. I asked journalist Elena Valeriote, who is based in Tuscany and specializes in agricultural and environmental issues, for tips on more eco-friendly stuzzichini-ing, both out in the world, and right at home. Here's what she had to say:

ON-PREMISES APERITIVO

* "Be sure to order your cocktail without a straw; alternatively, bring your own reusable one, or seek out bars that use compostable straws.

* "Opt for bars where drinks are served in glasses, rather than plastic cups.

* "Ask about the stuzzichini that are offered or take a look at what everyone around you is enjoying. If there's something you won't eat, let the server know not to bring it to the table! (Avoid food waste whenever possible.)

* "Start a conversation with your bartender or server. Ask about where the stuzzichini ingredients come from and request organic and local products whenever possible.

* "Seek out locally produced stuzzichini and aperitivo drinks in order to minimize your carbon footprint and support your local community."

AT-HOME APERITIVO

* "Avoid single-use plastics.

* "Opt for seasonal, local takes on stuzzichini classics. The ingredients don't need to come from Italy! Get curious about what kind of salty snacks, pickles, cheeses, meats, and breads can be sourced nearby. The local farmers market is a great place to start.

* "Aim to use ingredients that consume minimal water during the production process and support soil health. Instead of almonds and other nuts that traditionally satisfy the salty, crunchy part of aperitivo, consider legumes such as brined lupini, crispy peas, raw fava beans, and roasted chickpeas.

* "Transform last night's dinner leftovers into tonight's stuzzichini to avoid food waste. That final piece of stale bread can be given new life by pan-frying it in olive oil, while small portions of other leftover food, like cooked vegetables, can be pureed into a simple spread. Serve together as crostini."

Suggested Menus

The following are a few ideas for full tasting menus composed of stuzzichini, drawing from different sections of the book and taking into account flavor profiles, textures, preparation times, and host demands. This should help ensure you don't spend time overthinking, and allow you to prioritize moments with your guests.

The Glory of Butter

There are some who might exclusively think of olive oil as the nation's preferred source of fat. But what Italy can do with butter—particularly in northern regions— is nothing short of miraculous. This menu is for the lipid curious, and the legions of butter lovers everywhere.

POPCORN ALLA SALVIA & BURRO BRUNO
Sage and Brown Butter Popcorn
(PAGE 27)

CRACKER DI POLENTA AL BURRO BRUNO
Brown Butter Polenta Crackers
(PAGE 32)

GNUDI DI SPINACI CROCCANTI FRITTI IN PADELLA
Crispy Pan-Fried Spinach Gnudi
(PAGE 156)

ACCIUGHE CON BURRO & LIMONE
Anchovy Toast with Butter and Lemon
(PAGE 106)

TRAMEZZINI AL BURRO DI POMODORO
Tomato Butter Finger Sandwiches
(PAGE 129)

ALBICOCCHE AL FORNO
Oven Roasted Apricots
(PAGE 67)

Summer and Spring

The warmer seasons in Italy, when the markets have come back to life and everyone has absolutely had it with being indoors, are thrilling. Market tables spill with tender bundles of asparagus and wicker baskets of fava beans, fruit vendors cut slices of fresh peaches for samples because they know that with one taste, the tart, juicy thing will sell itself. This menu makes the most of spring and summer produce, no matter where you happen to be.

ASPARAGI ARROTOLATI CON PANCETTA
Roasted Asparagus Bundles with Pancetta **(PAGE 52)**

"CANNOLI" DI MELANZANE
Eggplant "Cannoli" **(PAGE 53)**

CROSTINI DI PATÉ DI FAVE
Fava Bean Pate Crostini **(PAGE 119)**

SPIEDINI DI POMODORO FRAGOLA BASILICO
Tomato and Strawberry Basil Skewers **(PAGE 84)**

CROSTONE DI SARDINE CON PESCHE & FINOCCHIO
Sardine Crostone with Peach and Fennel **(PAGE 116)**

GELO DI MELONE
Sicilian Watermelon Pudding **(PAGE 204)**

SGROPPINO AL LIMONE
—cocktail **(PAGE 244)**

Winter and Fall

Hearty roots and roasty vegetables reign supreme when the summer finally comes to its end. The holiday season is marked by the aroma of vin brulé, and by the time the New Year rolls around there's no better way to celebrate than with caldarroste. Italians are also famous for stashing away their most precious produce for the colder seasons, so even tomatoes come back to life on this menu, a preservation of the Mediterranean sun in its most concentrated form.

FUNGHI RIPIENI CON DATTERI & 'NDUJA
Mushrooms Stuffed with Dates and 'Nduja
(PAGE 48)

CROSTINI DI ESTRATTO DI POMODORO ALLE ERBE
Tomato Paste Crostini with Herbs
(PAGE 117)

INDIVIA CON CREMA DI GORGONZOLA DOLCE,
MELA & NOCE
Endive with Sweet Gorgonzola Cream,
Apple, and Walnut
(PAGE 63)

CALDARROSTE
Roasted Chestnuts
(PAGE 35)

VIN BRULÉ
—cocktail
(PAGE 247)

Northern Exposure

The top half of the boot is often overlooked in favor of its postcard-worthy regional relatives in the south, but northern Italy has loads to celebrate all year long—and not just its hazelnuts or world-class wines and chocolates. This menu plots a course through the Italian Alps and surrounding regions, and invites guests to reconsider the identity of the peninsula's diverse food.

FAGOTTINI DI SPECK & FORMAGGIO
Speck and Cheese Bundles
(PAGE 49)

GIRELLE DI RADICCHIO BRASATO AL VERMOUTH
CON ARANCIA & CIPOLLA ROSSA
Vermouth-Braised Radicchio Girelle with
Orange and Red Onion
(PAGE 62)

CROSTINI AL FORMAGGIO LIPTAUER CON
RAVANELLO & ERBA CIPOLLINA
Liptauer Cheese with Radish and Chive Toasts
(PAGE 137)

TORTA DI PATATE DI TRENTINO
Trentino Potato Pancake
(PAGE 164)

BOMBARDINO
—cocktail
(PAGE 243)

Seafood

Seafood culture is present in one form or another in every one of Italy's twenty regions. While this menu draws from various parts of Italy, the recipes are adaptable to availability in your own local region, and will please any crowd with a predilection for swimmers.

ACCIUGHE CON BURRO & LIMONE
Anchovy Toast with Butter and Lemon **(PAGE 106)**

**BISCOTTI SALATI CON MOUSSE
DI SALMONE AFFUMICATO**
Salty Biscuits with Smoked Salmon Mousse
(PAGE 28)

SPIEDINI DI GAMBERI AL PESTO ROSSO
Red Pesto Shrimp Spiedini
(PAGE 86)

CROSTINI DE BACCALÀ MANTECATO
Salt Cod Crostini
(PAGE 125)

SARDINE FRITTE
Fried Sardines **(PAGE 175)**

**CROCCHETTE DI GRANCHIO CON
VINAIGRETTE AGLI AGRUMI STREGA**
Crab Fritters with Strega Citrus Vinaigrette
(PAGE 186)

PONCE LIVORNESE
—cocktail
(PAGE 241)

Frutta Secca and Honey

There are dishes in Italy that are a trail mix lover's dream. Dried fruits and nuts (both of which fall under the description *frutta secca,* which literally translates as "dried fruit") show up all over the country, in preparations both sweet and savory, at all times of day. For a country that wastes nothing and preserves skillfully, these ingredients are prized and precious—not to mention utterly delicious.

GIRELLE DI RADICCHIO BRASATO AL VERMOUTH
CON ARANCIA & CIPOLLA ROSSA
Vermouth-Braised Radicchio Girelle with
Orange and Red Onion **(PAGE 62)**

FICHI AL FORNO
Oven Roasted Figs
(PAGE 66)

CAPRA & GRANA PALLINI CON
MELOGRANO & ARANCIA
Goat and Grana Padano Balls with
Pomegranate and Orange
(PAGE 75)

SPIEDINI DI MAIALE & DATTERI ALLE ERBE
Pork and Date Herb Skewers with
Spiced Orange Glaze
(PAGE 81)

CROSTINI DI FRUTTA DI STAGIONE,
RICOTTA, MIELE & PROSCIUTTO
Crostini with Seasonal Fruit, Ricotta, and Honey
(PAGE 120)

GIUGGIULENA
Sicilian Sesame Brittle
(PAGE 209)

PINEAPPLE GARIBALDI
—cocktail
(PAGE 218)

Herbs and Citrus

I have often heard it said that Italian cooks can work magic with a squeeze of lemon and a leaf of basil, and I have found that to be unequivocally true. That said, there are a lot of variations on that theme, and this menu makes good use of the country's diverse products in both categories.

FOCACCINE DI ROSMARINO & LARDO
Rosemary and Lardo Focaccine
(PAGE 108)

PIADINE CON TALEGGIO & PORCINI
Porcini and Taleggio Piadine
(PAGE 130)

MOZZARELLA IN CARROZZA AL PESTO
Mozzarella in a Carriage with Pesto
(PAGE 176)

BISCOTTI DI HUGO
Hugo Cookies
(PAGE 206)

BASIL GRAPEFRUIT HUGO
—cocktail
(PAGE 232)

Vegan

Sometimes, having parameters can encourage immense creativity, but creating a menu sans meat and dairy is actually not a huge challenge for the aperitivo host. Stuzzichini—and Italian food in general—are very friendly to dietary restrictions and preferences, thanks to a natural focus on vegetables and economy. This menu presents a collection of those kinds of dishes, but pulls no punches when it comes to flavors, textures, and overall satisfaction.

PATATE AL FORNO CON ROSMARINO & SALE
Oven Roasted Potatoes with Rosemary and Sea Salt
(VEGAN, GF, PAGE 76)

POMODORI MARINATI
Marinated Tomatoes
(VEGAN, GF, PAGE 87)

OLIVE AL FORNO
Oven Roasted Olives
(VEGAN, GF, PAGE 80)

SALVIA FRITTA NELLA BIRRA
Beer-Battered Sage Leaves
(VEGAN, PAGE 174)

TORTA DI CECI AL SALE MARINO & OLIO D'OLIVA
Sea Salt and Olive Oil Chickpea Pancake
(VEGAN, GF, PAGE 167)

PANE CON TAPENADE DI CIOCCOLATO
Chocolate Tapenade Toasts
(VEGAN, PAGE 145)

SORBETTO ALLA VANIGLIA APEROL
Aperol Vanilla Sorbet
(VEGAN [WITHOUT WHIPPED CREAM GARNISH], GF, PAGE 203)

CLASSIC SPRITZ
—or a customized riff
(PAGE 229)

Acknowledgments

In the true spirit of aperitivo, this book is the result of a community coming together and sharing passions and talents so generously, and I am so humbled and grateful. A massive grazie mille to:

Mollie, my friend, my champion, my hero. Thank you for seeing and knowing me. I hope to always make you proud.

Michael Szczerban and Thea Diklich-Newell, for approaching this project with a true sense of heart, and for understanding what is special about Italian culture and people. Your genuine interest, thoughtful guidance, and unflagging support, as well as your own passion and purpose with Voracious, have been overwhelmingly inspiring. I'm honored to be a small part of it. To the many talented, generous humans at Voracious and Little, Brown who contributed to bringing this book to life and getting it out into the world, including Kirin Diemont, Pat Jalbert-Levine, Nyamekye Waliyaya, Katherine Akey, Jules Horbachevsky, Toni Tajima, Deri Reed, and Holly Hartman, a humble, hearty grazie mille.

Deepi, for being the best damn partner a human could dream of, for your vision and enthusiasm, your pronunciation of *stuzzichini*, and above all, your friendship. Three Negronis Deep and a lifetime more ahead.

EV, for letting me wallpaper our Florence apartment with Post-Its, for raising a Negroni with me to every achievement and/or knockdown, for tasting every cocktail, for listening to every ramble and reading every iteration, for loving Italy with such inspiring depth, and for loving me so well.

Tina & Vito, for giving me my first true experiences of Italian living, showing me the meaning of hospitality— and also for facilitating the predawn adventure that was this photo shoot. To la citta di Sabaudia, con amore.

The visual team: Adnan Saciragic, Zeke Goodwin, Emily Nolan. You all infused this book with more life and humanity than I could have imagined. The many recipe testers for extraordinary culinary talents and general gameness: Maite Gomez-Rejón, Ben Hunter, Benjamin Weiss & Talia Wachtel, Katie Bell & Andy Wooten, Diana Hossfeld, Ann Mesinger Swietnicki, Sarah Aranda, Donna Nayden, Ziza Bauer, Jeremy Arkin, Evan Price & Aubrey Dunham Price.

To the wonderful humans who provided resources and support, and fielded my zillion+ questions these past years: at Kromos, Luxardo, Anna Tasca Lanza, Katty Garcia & Gustavo Arias, Giulia Perovich, Laura Ruggieri & Hotel Maalot in Rome, Sacha Bell, Laura Zoff. To my professors at Lorenzo de Medici, including Lucia Soldi, Kate Bolton-Porciatti, and Alfredo Cisternino, who taught me Italian culture and history with passion and pride.

To those who lovingly shared expertise: Danielle Callegari, Nicole Dorigo, Ata De Çin, Emiko Davies, Simona Muratore. To those who shared their aperitivo experiences: Linda Foltran, Benedetta Cutolo, Elena Tina Maria Putignano, Henna Garrison,

Alexander Zeleniuch, Laura LaMonica, Alice Fischer. To Phoebe Hunt, for your coworking company, your spirit, your heart, and your meaningful friendship.

To the people of Florence who welcomed me into their community (during a global pandemic, no less), and all over Italy. To the folks at Ditta Artigianale, who furnished the many, many espresso drinks that fueled the creation of this book. To the teachers at Parola Scuola di Lingua Italiana for imbuing every word with magic.

To Nonny & Grandpa, for setting me on this path the moment you started your own journeys from Patrica and Veroli. To Rose & Kev, for literally everything, always. To the cousins, to Dan & Bridget, to Lucy, Scarlett, and Ava and the next gen. To Bernie, Donna, and the fam for your interest and enthusiasm.

And to my community—you all are what this book is about: Gia, Farrin, Ben, Cash & Izaac, Katie & Andy, Collin & Joe, Lindsay & Brian, Maite & Dave, Antonio, Louis & Beth, Onnesha, Jeremy, Katrina, Diana, Brian & Ashley, Andy & Hannah, Ben & Talia, Patrick & Rachel, Evan & Aubrey, Jarred & Ashley, Jonas & Lauryn, Julie G., Jess & Trina, Umber, Fany, and the Valeriote family.

Index

Note: Page references in *italics* indicate recipe photographs.

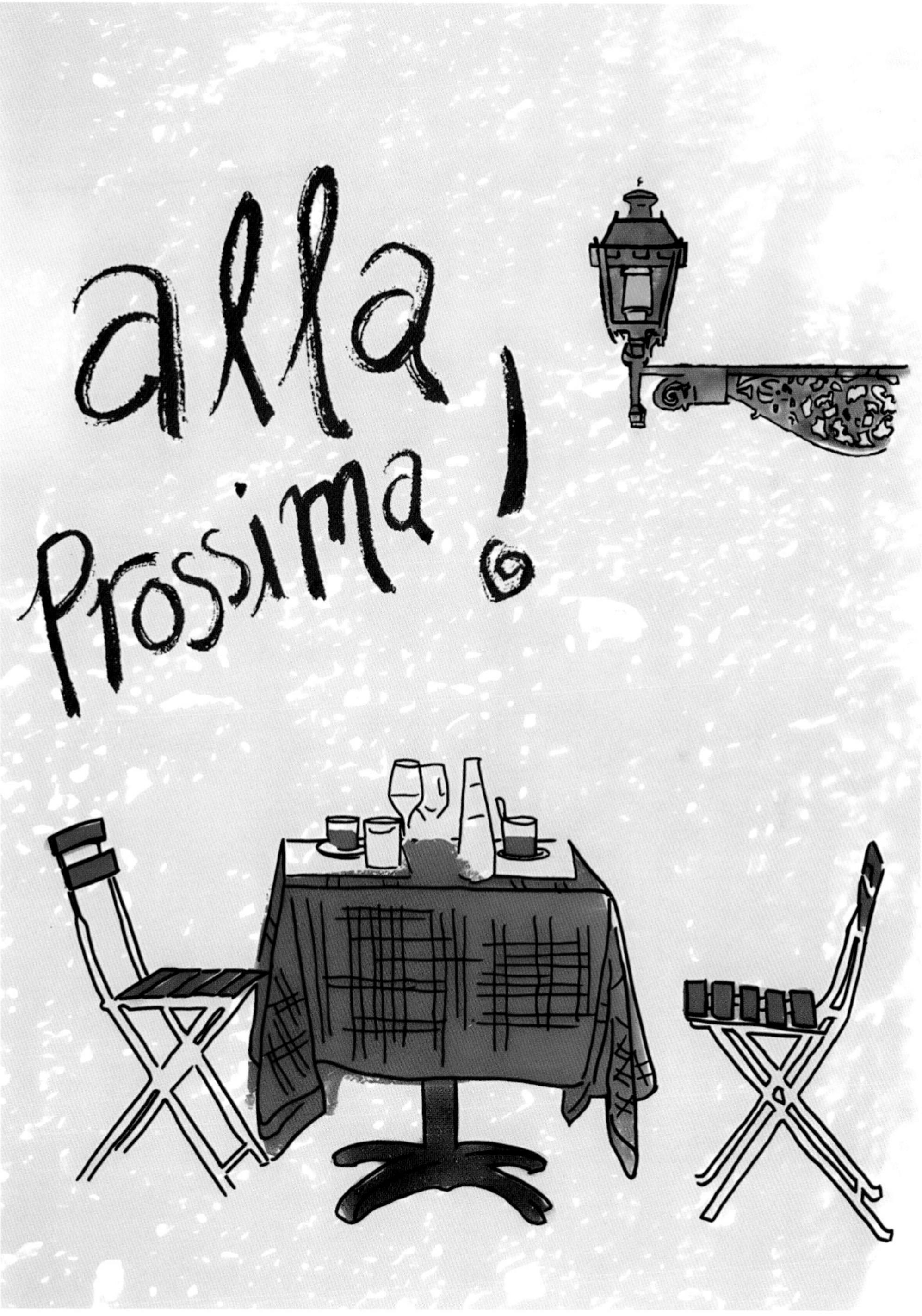
alla
Prossima!

About the Author

Stef Ferrari is a three-time Emmy-winning, James Beard Award–nominated producer on the PBS docuseries *The Migrant Kitchen*. She served as senior editor at *Life & Thyme* and is the author or coauthor of several books, including *Ice Cream Adventures*, Aarón Sánchez's *Where I Come From*, and Voracious's own *A Woman's Place*. A certified Cicerone (beer sommelier) and food culture journalist and educator, she has lived in and traveled throughout Italy, sampling the best of regional stuzzichini.